# FEARLESSENCE

Copyright © 2024 by A.J. Solano

All rights reserved. No part of this book may be reproduced in any manner whatsoever without written permission except in the case of brief quotations embodied in critical articles and reviews.

First Printing, 2024

# FearLESSence

A.J. Solano

# CONTENTS

Welcome to the No-F#ck Zone . . . . . . . . . . vii

- Part 1: The Mental Mess . . . . . . . . 1
1 - Fear of Being Judged . . . . . . . . 3
2 - Imposter Syndrome . . . . . . . . 9
3 - Perfectionism . . . . . . . . 15
4 - Fear of Failure . . . . . . . . 21
5 - Self-Doubt . . . . . . . . 27
6 - Overthinking . . . . . . . . 33
7 - Procrastination . . . . . . . . 39
8 - Fear of Success . . . . . . . . 45
9 - Comparison Trap . . . . . . . . 51
10 - Approval Addiction . . . . . . . . 57
- Part 2: Social Survival . . . . . . . . 65
11 - Social Anxiety . . . . . . . . 67
12 - Fear of Rejection . . . . . . . . 73
13 - Loneliness . . . . . . . . 79
14 - Being Too Much or Not Enough . . . . . 87
15 - Body Image . . . . . . . . 95

| | | |
|---|---|---|
| 16 – | Fear of Intimacy | 103 |
| 17 – | People-Pleasing | 111 |
| 18 – | Toxic Relationships | 117 |
| 19 – | Need for Control | 125 |
| 20 – | Fear of Confrontation | 133 |
| – | Part 3: Owning Your Sh#t | 141 |
| 21 – | Self-Worth | 143 |
| 22 – | FOMO (Fear of Missing Out) | 151 |
| 23 – | Fear of Change | 159 |
| 24 – | Guilt and Shame | 167 |
| 25 – | Perceived Weakness | 175 |
| 26 – | The Need to Be Liked | 183 |
| 27 – | Lack of Motivation | 191 |
| 28 – | Fear of Being Yourself | 199 |
| 29 – | Saying F#ck It | 207 |

The Final F#ck . . . . . . . . . . . . . . . . . . . . . 215

# WELCOME TO THE NO-F#CK ZONE

So, you're here because you're tired of giving too many f#cks. Maybe you're exhausted from pretending to be someone else, hoping the world will finally approve of you. Or maybe your inner critic's a loudmouth that won't shut up, telling you you're not good enough, smart enough, skinny enough, *anything* enough. Whatever it is, let's cut the crap—you're ready to change. But not the "let's all sing kumbaya" kind of change. Nope. This is the gritty, raw, "I'm f#cking done caring" kind of change.

Here's the truth: insecurities suck. They drain your energy, hijack your peace of mind, and make life feel like one giant obstacle course where the finish line keeps moving. They sneak up on you in the most ridiculous ways—like when you second-guess every single word in a group text or obsess over whether your laugh is too weird for public consumption. But don't worry, you're not alone. The world is full of people tripping over their own insecurities, acting like they've got their sh#t together when, really, they're just hoping no one notices how hard they're sweating.

In this book, we're going to get real—real messy, real uncomfortable, and real f#cking free. You're going to laugh (at yourself, mostly), cringe (probably a lot), and, most importantly, you're going to let go of the fears that have been holding you hostage. We'll unpack the insecurities that have kept you playing small and dissect why you've been handing out f#cks like free samples. Then, we'll set fire to all that sh#t and build something better.

This isn't about becoming someone you're not; it's about reclaiming who you are—unapologetically. No more wasting energy trying to fit into someone else's mold. No more seeking approval from people who don't matter. And no more drowning in self-doubt like it's a f#cking lifestyle. *FearLESSence* is your permission slip to show up exactly as you are—flaws, quirks, awkwardness, and all. Because the real power comes when you stop giving a f#ck and start living for yourself.

So, buckle up, buttercup. It's time to ditch the mental BS, tell your insecurities to f#ck off, and start owning your damn life. You in? Let's do this.

# PART 1: THE MENTAL MESS

# 1

# FEAR OF BEING JUDGED

Let's start with one of the biggest killers of confidence: the fear of being judged. You know the drill. You walk into a room, instantly convinced that everyone is staring at you, silently scrutinizing your every move—like you're the main act in some judgment circus. Whether it's what you're wearing, how you're walking, or the way you nearly trip over your own feet, it feels like all eyes are on you, picking apart your flaws one by one. News flash: they're not. Seriously, no one cares that much.

Here's the cold, hard truth: Most people are too wrapped up in their own sh#t to give much of a damn about you. They're busy worrying about their own awkwardness, insecurities, and embarrassing moments. If they are looking at you, it's probably for a split second before they go right back to obsessing over themselves. So why the hell do we keep living like we're on some kind of judgment stage? Spoiler alert: **it's all in your head**.

## THE GREAT EGO TRAP

The fear of being judged is a nasty side effect of our overinflated egos. Yep, you heard that right. It's not that we think we're all that, but we secretly believe we're important enough for everyone to have an opinion about us. News flash #2: We're not. Imagine this—you walk into a party, and there's this invisible spotlight following you around. You're positive that people are dissecting your outfit, your hair, your weird laugh. But what if that spotlight doesn't exist? What if it's just your own mental trick to make you think you're more important than you are?

It's not that people are cruel or out to judge you—they're just not that interested. Let that sink in for a moment. Feels liberating, right? The truth is, most of us are living in our own little bubbles of self-obsession, thinking the world is constantly watching us when in reality, everyone's just trying to survive the same sh#tstorm of insecurities.

## THE MYTH OF PERFECTION

Now let's tackle why this fear sticks around: perfectionism. Somehow, we've been conditioned to believe that if we're not flawless, we'll be exposed, judged, and possibly exiled from society. It's like we're terrified that one awkward moment is going to be our undoing. But guess what? Perfection is a lie, a myth we tell ourselves to justify the exhausting charade of trying to be "good enough."

Here's the kicker: even if someone *does* judge you, what does that really say about them? People who spend their time tearing others down are usually drowning in their own sea of insecurities. Their opinions? They matter about as much as a fart in the wind—fleeting and full of hot air. Trust me, their judgment has way more to do with them than it does with you.

### THE MAGIC OF GIVING FEWER F#CKS

Imagine what life would look like if you gave fewer f#cks about other people's opinions. Seriously, take a moment to visualize it. You'd show up to that party wearing whatever the hell you want, talk to strangers without replaying every word in your head afterward, and maybe—just maybe—you'd stop contorting yourself into a version of "you" that's designed to please the masses.

The magic happens when you realize that the only person whose opinion matters is *yours*. And the truth is, your life gets exponentially better when you start caring about what *you* think, not what some random bystander might be whispering under their breath (which, again, they're probably not). When you live authentically, people gravitate toward you—not because you're perfect, but because you're real.

### LET'S BREAK IT DOWN: WHY YOU SHOULD STOP GIVING A F#CK RIGHT NOW

1. **People Are Self-Absorbed** – Most people are too busy worrying about themselves to give your life a second thought. That "all eyes on me" feeling? It's just your mind playing games.
2. **Judgment Is Temporary** – Even if someone *does* judge you, their opinion is like a fart: noticeable

for a second and then gone. It doesn't leave a lasting impact unless you let it.
3. **Perfection Isn't Real** – You'll never be "perfect," and that's the best news ever. The sooner you accept that, the sooner you can stop bending over backward trying to be something you're not.
4. **Their Opinion Isn't Your Business** – Other people's opinions are a reflection of *them*, not you. So, unless someone's opinion is going to pay your bills or add years to your life, why care?
5. **Freedom Is Authenticity** – The moment you start being unapologetically yourself is the moment you stop being a prisoner to the fear of judgment. The people who matter will love you for you; the rest can f#ck right off.

**YOUR HOMEWORK: THE F#CK-IT EXPERIMENT**

This week, I want you to run an experiment. Find a situation where you'd normally freak out about being judged—maybe it's going to the gym in an old, mismatched outfit, speaking up in a meeting, or dancing like a maniac at a party. Now, here's the trick: before you go into it, remind yourself that no one's really paying that much attention. Go in with that mindset and see what happens.

Chances are, no one will judge you. And if they do, remind yourself that their opinion doesn't matter. The goal is to prove to yourself that the world isn't actually watching, and even if they are, their judgments won't kill you. By the end of this experiment, you'll have irrefutable evidence that people's opinions are as irrelevant as you suspected.

**FINAL THOUGHT**

The fear of being judged isn't some permanent condition you're doomed to suffer from. It's a habit, a mental reflex, and—like any habit—it can be broken. All it takes is a little perspective and a lot fewer f#cks given. So the next time you catch yourself spiraling into a pit of "what will they think of me?" pause and ask yourself, "Are they really thinking about me, or am I just *assuming* they are?"

Answer: They're not.

# 2

# IMPOSTER SYNDROME

So, you've done the thing. You got the promotion, nailed the presentation, or finally hit a major life goal. You should be feeling on top of the world, right? Wrong. Instead, you're sitting there thinking, *They're gonna figure me out.* You're convinced it's all been a fluke and any second now, someone's going to walk up, rip off your "I'm competent" mask, and shout, "Aha! I knew it! You're a fraud!"

Welcome to **Imposter Syndrome**—that charming little mental monster that shows up the moment you achieve something and tries to convince you it was all luck, that you didn't deserve it, and that eventually, everyone's going to find out you have no idea what the hell you're doing. The funny thing is, the more successful you are, the louder this voice gets. The better you do, the more you feel like a fraud.

Here's the twist: feeling like a fraud doesn't mean you're failing; it actually means you're pushing your limits. You're doing something right. So how do you shut down that inner imposter and own your badassery? Let's dive into the mess of it.

## WHY YOUR BRAIN IS BEING A JERK

Imposter syndrome thrives on one basic lie: *You're not good enough.* Even when you have a stack of accomplishments taller than your laundry pile, your brain loves to downplay every win and amplify every screw-up. You tell yourself you're not "really" qualified for your job, or you don't "actually" know what you're doing in that relationship, or that whatever good thing happened was a lucky accident.

But here's the thing: that voice in your head is full of sh#t. It's the brain's way of keeping you in your comfort zone—where you're safe, small, and conveniently not at risk of being exposed as a "fraud." See, imposter syndrome is like a crappy security system. It goes off every time you step out of your usual boundaries, even though there's no real threat. It's trying to protect you, but it's just annoying the hell out of you instead.

## THE HIGH ACHIEVER'S CURSE

Ever notice that the most successful people are often the ones who feel like frauds? That's because the more you achieve, the bigger your world gets, and the more you're exposed to stuff you *don't* know. As you climb higher, the stakes get bigger, and your self-doubt does, too. The reality is, imposter syndrome doesn't show up because you're unqualified—it shows up because you're leveling up. And that's a damn good thing.

Imposter syndrome is your mind's awkward way of telling you that you're breaking new ground, stepping into places you haven't been before. You're expanding, which means you don't have all the answers. That's not fraud; that's growth. It's okay not to know everything. It's okay to feel out of your depth. You're learning, you're stretching, and you're getting better—whether that annoying voice in your head believes it or not.

**EVERYONE FEELS IT—EVEN THE "GREATS"**

Think this is just your personal mess? Nope. Even the most successful people you can think of have wrestled with imposter syndrome. Maya Angelou, one of the most respected writers in history, once said, "I have written eleven books, but each time I think, 'Uh oh, they're going to find out now. I've run a game on everybody, and they're going to find me out.'" That's Maya Angelou—an absolute legend. If she can feel like a fraud, you're in good company.

Imposter syndrome isn't a reflection of your abilities; it's just part of the human condition. We all carry self-doubt, but the trick is not letting it control the narrative. The real frauds out there? They don't feel imposter syndrome. They walk around with undeserved confidence, bluffing their way through life without a second thought. Meanwhile, you, with your actual talent, are sweating bullets thinking you're a fake. The irony is painfully hilarious.

**WHY YOU'RE MORE THAN QUALIFIED**

Let's dismantle the fraud complex with some cold, hard facts:

1. **You've Done the Work** – You didn't just wake up one day and stumble into your current position, career, or accomplishment. You put in the hours, the effort, and the sweat to get where you are. That wasn't luck. It was hustle.
2. **Others Believe in You** – Someone gave you that job, that opportunity, or that role for a reason. Unless they're legally blind, they saw your value and trusted you to handle it. If they believe in you, why can't you?
3. **You're Learning as You Go** – No one has it all figured out. Not even the experts. The difference between them and the rest? They keep learning and adapting along the way. You don't need to know everything on day one. Give yourself some damn credit.
4. **You're Not Alone** – Everyone—literally *everyone*—has felt like they're faking it at some point. It's normal. You're not broken; you're just human. And you're in great company.

**KICKING THE IMPOSTER TO THE CURB**

Now that we've established you're not actually a fraud, let's talk about how to silence that inner critic when it tries to tell you otherwise:

1. **Collect the Receipts** – Keep track of your wins. Make a list of every accomplishment, every time you nailed something, and every compliment or recognition you've received. This isn't about feeding your ego—it's about creating a defense file to slap that imposter syndrome in the face when it rears its ugly head.

2. **Talk to Yourself Like a Friend** – You wouldn't tell your best friend they're a fraud, so why do you say that to yourself? Next time imposter syndrome creeps in, flip the script. Imagine you're talking to someone you care about, and give yourself the same pep talk you'd give them.
3. **Get Comfortable With Discomfort** – The feeling of being out of your depth isn't a sign you're failing; it's a sign you're growing. Get cozy with being uncomfortable. It's proof that you're leveling up.
4. **Own Your Sh#t** – When someone compliments you or acknowledges your work, resist the urge to deflect. Don't minimize it. Say "thank you" and let it sink in. You've earned it.

**YOUR HOMEWORK: THE ANTI-IMPOSTER LOG**

For the next week, I want you to start a simple but powerful habit: the Anti-Imposter Log. At the end of each day, write down at least one thing you did well. It could be anything—big or small—that shows you're *not* a fraud. It could be a task you completed, a compliment you received, or even a situation where you kept your cool when things went to sh#t. By the end of the week, you'll have a stack of evidence proving that imposter syndrome is full of it.

**FINAL THOUGHT**

Imposter syndrome isn't going to magically disappear overnight. It's a persistent little bastard that loves to show up whenever you're stepping outside your comfort zone. But here's the thing: feeling like a fraud means you're growing. It means you're doing things that scare you, and that's exactly where you need to be. So next time you feel that voice whispering "You don't belong here," remind yourself—yes, you f#cking do. And you're only just getting started.

# 3

# PERFECTIONISM

Let's get real about perfectionism, shall we? You know that exhausting, never-satisfied feeling that no matter how much you do, it's never quite *enough*? That's perfectionism, like a silent stalker, always hovering in the background of your life, whispering, *"You could have done better."* Whether it's your work, relationships, or even how well you cook scrambled eggs, perfectionism makes you feel like you're always coming up short.

Here's the kicker: **perfect doesn't exist.** It's a made-up fairy tale, like unicorns or the idea that you can eat just one potato chip. Yet, perfectionism convinces you that if you just work harder, stay up later, or tweak things a little more, you'll finally reach that mythical finish line. Spoiler alert—there's no finish line. Perfectionism is a hamster wheel of endless effort, and it's time to jump off before it grinds you into dust.

### THE UGLY TRUTH ABOUT PERFECTIONISM

At its core, perfectionism is a coping mechanism. It's how we try to protect ourselves from criticism, failure, and—wait for it—judgment. If we're perfect, then no one can attack us, right? If everything's flawless, we'll be loved, admired, and never have to feel like the messy, vulnerable humans we are. Sounds good in theory, but in reality, it's a load of bullsh#t.

Perfectionism doesn't protect you; it imprisons you. Instead of freeing you from fear, it amplifies it. You become so afraid of making mistakes, of not measuring up, that you end up paralyzed. You don't take risks, you avoid putting yourself out there, and you beat yourself up for every minor slip-up. Worse, perfectionism is sneaky. It disguises itself as ambition, making you think you're just striving for excellence. But in reality, it's sabotaging your happiness.

**THE PERFECTIONIST'S PLAYBOOK**

Recognize any of these?

- **"It has to be flawless, or it's worthless."**
  You can't bring yourself to finish that project because it's not 100% perfect, so instead, you keep tinkering with it—or worse, you don't finish it at all.
- **"I'll never be good enough."**
  Even when you do well, you immediately dismiss it as "lucky" or "not that great," convincing yourself that someone else could have done it better.
- **"If I fail, everyone will know I'm a fraud."**
  Failure feels like proof that you're not just imperfect but fundamentally unworthy. So, you avoid anything that might lead to it—even if it means missing out on opportunities.

- **"I can't rest until everything's done."**
You can't enjoy your downtime because there's always more to do, more to fix, more to perfect. Fun? What's that?

Does any of that sound like excellence to you? Nope. That's perfectionism lying to your face, making you believe you're striving for greatness when all you're really doing is spinning in circles.

## THE COST OF CHASING PERFECTION

Perfectionism has a hefty price tag, and it's not just your sanity. It costs you your creativity, your joy, and your ability to grow. When you're obsessed with being perfect, you stop experimenting. You stop trying new things because *what if you suck at them?* You play it safe because failure feels like the ultimate disaster. And in the process, you miss out on the messy, imperfect magic that makes life interesting.

Oh, and spoiler: nobody likes a perfectionist. When you're constantly holding yourself to an impossible standard, you tend to hold others to it, too. This turns you into the fun-sucking control freak who stresses out over the tiniest details and loses their sh#t when things don't go according to plan. Perfectionism doesn't just ruin your mood; it drags everyone else down with you.

## EMBRACING THE MESS: THE ANTIDOTE TO PERFECTIONISM

You want to know what's better than perfect? **Real.** Real is messy, unpredictable, and flawed. Real is the human experience. The moment you stop chasing flawless and start embracing the chaos, your life gets a whole lot better—and a lot more fun. Here's how to kick perfectionism in the ass and start embracing the beautifully imperfect chaos of your life:

1. **Redefine Success**
   Perfectionism tricks you into thinking success means doing everything perfectly, but real success is about *progress*, not perfection. Did you show up? Did you put in the effort? Did you learn something? That's success. Forget about perfect outcomes and focus on growth.
2. **Celebrate the Flaws**
   Perfectionists hate making mistakes, but mistakes are where the magic happens. They're where you learn, grow, and get better. So, when you screw up (and you will), take a moment to appreciate the lesson. It means you're trying, which is far more valuable than staying in your safe little bubble.
3. **Adopt the "Good Enough" Rule**
   This might feel like blasphemy, but sometimes, "good enough" is just that—enough. When you're working on a project, don't aim for flawless. Aim for *done*. Most of the time, what you think is "good enough" is more than enough for everyone else.
4. **Prioritize Rest and Fun**
   Perfectionists are notorious for burning themselves

out in the pursuit of excellence. But guess what? You're not a f#cking robot. You need rest. You need fun. You need to step away from the grind and recharge. Let yourself relax. The world isn't going to implode if you take a break.
5. **Surround Yourself with Imperfection**
Look at the people in your life who embrace their flaws, who take risks, who laugh at their own mistakes. These are your new role models. Spend time with people who aren't obsessed with being perfect, and watch how they live fully, without fear of failure. Let that energy rub off on you.

**YOUR HOMEWORK: THE "F#CK IT" PROJECT**

This week, pick one thing that you've been obsessively tweaking, delaying, or avoiding because it's "not perfect." Now, here's the deal: you're going to finish it, imperfect as it may be. Don't aim for flawless—aim for *done*. Whether it's sending that email, finishing that art project, or finally posting that photo on Instagram, your job is to get it out there, imperfections and all.

Once it's done, *don't* go back and analyze it. Don't pick it apart. Let it live in all its messy glory, and then move the hell on. The goal here is to prove to yourself that perfection isn't necessary, and sometimes, "good enough" really is more than enough.

**FINAL THOUGHT**

Perfectionism is a myth, a trap that keeps you stuck in a never-ending loop of self-criticism and dissatisfaction. The truth is, life is messy, and that's what makes it beautiful. When you stop trying to control every little detail and embrace the chaos, you free yourself to actually *live*—flaws, failures, and all. So, here's to being beautifully imperfect. After all, the only thing perfect about life is its unpredictability. Let's f#cking embrace it.

# 4

# FEAR OF FAILURE

Let's cut to the chase: failure is inevitable. I know, not exactly what you want to hear, but it's the truth. No matter how much you plan, prepare, or pray to the gods of success, you're going to fall flat on your face more times than you can count. And that's a good thing. The ugly truth about life is that failure is not just likely—it's necessary. If you're not failing, you're probably not doing anything worthwhile.

But here's the thing: failure isn't a death sentence. It's just a damn stepping stone, one you'll trip over, crash into, and maybe swear at a little. It's not the end of the road, it's just a pit stop on your way to something bigger. The problem is, most of us have been raised to fear failure like it's the plague. We're taught to avoid it at all costs, like one screw-up will permanently define us as losers. That's bullsh#t. Failure doesn't define you—how you handle it does.

## WHY WE FEAR FAILURE SO DAMN MUCH

Let's break down why failure freaks us the f#ck out. It's not the actual act of failing that terrifies us; it's what we think failure *means*. We equate failure with shame, embarrassment, and the death of our self-worth. Somewhere along the way, we got it into our heads that failing makes us less valuable. We're convinced that people will judge us, laugh at us, or worse, abandon us. But here's the kicker: that fear is based on a myth.

Failure doesn't mean you suck. It doesn't mean you're unworthy, and it sure as hell doesn't mean you're done. It just means you tried something, and it didn't work out the way you planned. Big f#cking deal. Every successful person you've ever heard of has failed—probably more times than you've even tried. But they didn't let failure stop them; they used it to get better. That's the secret sauce.

## THE FAILURE FREAKOUT

Failure feels like sh#t in the moment because we tie our sense of identity to our accomplishments. When something goes wrong, we don't just think, *I failed at this task.* We think, *I am a failure.* It becomes personal, and that's where we mess ourselves up. But what if we stopped taking failure so personally? What if we saw it for what it really is—just feedback? What if we understood that failing is simply part of the process, like the universe's way of saying, *Nice try, now try again—differently.*

Failure is a teacher, not a judge. It's not here to condemn you; it's here to course-correct you. Every failure brings you one step closer to getting it right, but only if you're willing to pick yourself up and learn the damn lesson.

## THE GREATS? THEY FAILED MORE THAN YOU

You think successful people are just lucky, gifted, or somehow immune to failure? Think again. They've failed so many times it would make your head spin. Take Thomas Edison, for example. That dude failed *thousands* of times before he got the lightbulb right. When asked about his failures, he didn't throw in the towel—he famously said, "I have not failed. I've just found 10,000 ways that won't work."

And what about J.K. Rowling? Before *Harry Potter* made her a billionaire, she was rejected by twelve publishers. Twelve. They probably feel like total a##holes now. But she didn't give up; she kept going. The difference between people who succeed and people who don't isn't talent—it's persistence. Successful people don't let failure stop them; they let it fuel them. They understand that failure is just part of the journey, not the end of the road.

## FAILURE: THE STEPPING STONE TO GREATNESS

Here's the f#cking truth: failure is the price of admission for success. If you want to do anything meaningful in life, you're going to fail—a lot. But every time you fail, you're one step closer to figuring sh#t out. You're refining your approach, learning what doesn't work, and getting better every time. Failure is not the opposite of success; it's a prerequisite.

Think about learning to walk. As a baby, you fell over hundreds of times before you finally got the hang of it. But did you quit and think, *I guess walking just isn't for me*? Hell no. You kept getting up and trying again. And guess what? Eventually, you nailed it. It's the same with everything else in life. Whether it's starting a business, asking someone out, or learning a new skill, you're going to suck at first. But failure isn't final unless you decide to stop trying.

**HOW TO FAIL LIKE A BOSS**

So, how do you start seeing failure as a stepping stone instead of a dead end? Here's how to fail like a boss:

1. **Detach from the Outcome**
   Your worth is not tied to whether or not something works out. Failure is an event, not an identity. You failed at something, but *you* are not a failure. Learn to separate the two, and you'll take the sting out of failure.
2. **Embrace the F#ck-Ups**
   Stop running from failure and start seeing it as part of the process. Expect to fail, and when it happens, don't freak out—embrace it. Ask yourself, *What did I learn?* and use that to improve.
3. **Fail Fast and Move On**
   Don't dwell on failure. When something goes wrong, take the lesson, adjust your strategy, and keep moving forward. The longer you wallow, the longer you're stuck in place. F#ck that. Fail fast, learn faster.
4. **Take Risks Anyway**
   The fear of failure stops most people from even try-

ing, but not you. Take the risk. Jump into the unknown. Yeah, you might fall on your face, but you'll get back up. And the reward? It's worth the fall every time.

5. **Find the Humor in It**
Failure can be brutal, but it's also pretty damn funny if you let it be. When things go wrong, laugh at the absurdity of it. Trust me, your future self will look back on those "failures" and see them for the comedic gold they really are.

**YOUR HOMEWORK: THE F#CK-UP CHALLENGE**

This week, I want you to aim for failure. Yes, you heard that right. Find something you've been putting off because you're afraid of failing, and do it anyway. It could be starting that side hustle, finally asking out your crush, or trying that intimidating workout routine. The goal isn't to avoid failure—it's to *expect* it. When things inevitably go wrong (and they will), I want you to write down what you learned from it.

The F#ck-Up Challenge isn't about success; it's about reframing your relationship with failure. It's about proving to yourself that failure isn't the end of the world—it's just another step forward. And hey, if you don't fail? Bonus points.

**FINAL THOUGHT**

The fear of failure is one of the biggest things holding you back from greatness. But here's the reality: failure is a fact of life. You're going to fail, and you're going to fail often. But guess what? That's okay. It's not about avoiding failure—it's about learning how to fail, get back up, and keep moving. Failure isn't the opposite of success; it's the road you have to take to get there. So, stop playing it safe, start embracing the f#ck-ups, and keep moving forward. Because the only true failure is never trying at all.

# 5

# SELF-DOUBT

There's a voice inside your head, and let's be honest—it's a bit of an a##hole. It's that nagging little voice that whispers, *Are you sure you can do this? What if you're not good enough? What if you fail and everyone finds out you're a fraud?* You know the one. It shows up right when you're on the verge of something big, something important, and it throws a giant wrench into your confidence, making you second-guess yourself at every turn.

Say hello to your **inner critic**, aka the source of 90% of your self-doubt. This persistent jerk shows up uninvited and always has something negative to say. But here's the truth: it's not just you. We all have an inner critic. The real issue isn't that it's there—it's that you've been letting it run the show. So, how do we shut this critic up and take back control? Buckle up, because we're about to put your inner critic in its place.

**THE ORIGINS OF YOUR INNER A##HOLE**

Self-doubt is a survival mechanism—left over from when our ancestors needed to avoid doing stupid things like poking saber-toothed tigers or jumping off cliffs. That little voice in our head was there to keep us cautious, which back then, made sense. But fast-forward to the present day, and now it's evolved into this constant, nagging stream of criticism that tells you not to take risks or put yourself out there. It's outdated software running in your brain, and it's time for an upgrade.

Your inner critic feeds on your fear of failure, rejection, and not being "enough." Every time you step out of your comfort zone, that voice gets louder, reminding you of every possible thing that could go wrong. But here's the thing—self-doubt isn't fact, it's fiction. It's a story your brain tells you, and most of the time, it's complete BS.

**THE CYCLE OF SELF-SABOTAGE**

Self-doubt is like a crappy little gremlin that sneaks in and wrecks everything. First, it gets you questioning whether you're good enough, smart enough, or talented enough. Then it makes you hesitate, procrastinate, and overanalyze. Finally, it pushes you into full-on paralysis, where you do absolutely nothing because you're too afraid to mess up. Sound familiar?

This is the cycle of self-sabotage:

1. **Self-doubt creeps in.**
2. **You overthink everything.**
3. **You hesitate or avoid taking action.**
4. **You confirm your worst fear by not succeeding**—not because you couldn't, but because you never gave yourself the chance to try.

5. **Rinse and repeat.**

It's a vicious loop that keeps you stuck in a pit of indecision and inaction. The longer you stay in it, the more you start to believe your own self-doubt. But here's the good news: that story is total fiction, and you have the power to rewrite it.

### REWRITING THE NARRATIVE

Self-doubt is a sneaky storyteller. It loves to weave together narratives based on fear, not fact. But the cool thing about stories is that they can be rewritten. You don't have to believe every negative thought that pops into your head. Just because your inner critic says something doesn't make it true. In fact, most of what it says is pure garbage. Time to shut that sh#t down and take control of the script.

Here's how to rewrite the self-sabotaging narrative your inner critic keeps feeding you:

1. **Call Out the BS**
   The next time your inner critic tells you, *You're not good enough*, pause and ask yourself, *Is that actually true?* Nine times out of ten, it's not. Challenge the thought. Where's the evidence that you're not good enough? More often than not, you'll find there isn't any.
2. **Flip the Script**
   Once you've called out the BS, replace it with a new, more empowering narrative. For example, instead of, *I'm not ready,* try, *I'm still learning, but I'm capable of*

*figuring it out.* Reframing the thought doesn't mean being delusional—it means giving yourself a fair shot.

3. **Treat Yourself Like a Friend**
Would you talk to your best friend the way your inner critic talks to you? Hell no. So why do you talk to yourself like that? Start treating yourself with the same kindness and understanding you'd give to someone you care about. When that critic pipes up, ask yourself, *What would I tell my friend in this situation?* Then say that to yourself.

4. **Stop Seeking External Validation**
Self-doubt often thrives on the need for validation from others. Here's a revolutionary idea: you don't need anyone's permission to believe in yourself. Confidence comes from within, not from someone else's approval. The moment you stop looking for validation outside yourself, your inner critic loses its power.

5. **Take Action Anyway**
Self-doubt hates action. The more you overthink, the louder that inner critic becomes. But when you start taking action—even imperfect action—that voice gets quieter. The key to overcoming self-doubt isn't to wait until you feel 100% confident. It's to take action despite the doubt. Confidence comes from doing, not thinking.

**WHY YOUR INNER CRITIC ISN'T ALWAYS WRONG**

Before you burn your inner critic at the stake, let's get one thing straight: sometimes, it's not entirely full of sh#t. The key is learning to tell the difference between helpful self-reflection and harmful self-doubt. Sometimes that little voice is actually offering you useful feedback—like,

*Hey, maybe don't quit your job and move to a commune just yet.* But most of the time, it's just playing defense to keep you from taking risks.

Instead of trying to silence your inner critic completely, learn to filter its input. Ask yourself: *Is this voice helping me improve, or is it just keeping me stuck?* If it's the latter, tell it to take a seat. But if it's offering constructive criticism, listen and learn—but don't let it dominate the conversation.

**OWNING YOUR SH#T**

At the end of the day, self-doubt is a self-imposed prison. You hold the key to getting out. It's all about learning to stop letting your inner critic run the show and start taking ownership of your narrative. You are more capable than you give yourself credit for, and the world is waiting for you to step up. Stop hiding behind your doubts and start stepping into your potential. It's time to own your sh#t.

**YOUR HOMEWORK: THE INNER CRITIC SHOWDOWN**

For the next week, I want you to start calling out your inner critic every time it pops up. When you catch yourself thinking, *I'm not good enough* or *I can't do this,* write that thought down. Then, challenge it. Ask yourself, *Is this true? Where's the evidence?* Once you've dismantled the negative thought, rewrite it into something more empowering.

This exercise isn't about blindly "thinking positive" (because that's just annoying). It's about recognizing when your inner critic is lying to you and replacing those lies with a more balanced truth. By the end of the week, you'll have a list of rewritten thoughts that you can refer to the next time self-doubt tries to take over.

**FINAL THOUGHT**

Self-doubt is just a story you've been telling yourself—and it's probably a boring, repetitive one. It's time to change the narrative. Your inner critic is always going to have something to say, but that doesn't mean you have to listen. Take control of the conversation, rewrite the script, and start believing in yourself. Because here's the truth: you're not only good enough, you're f#cking unstoppable—if you'd just get out of your own way. So tell your inner critic to shut the hell up, and go own your life.

# 6

# OVERTHINKING

Ah, overthinking—everyone's favorite mental torture device. If you're familiar with this gem, you know it well: that relentless loop of replaying every little thing you said, did, or thought, while your brain acts like an over-caffeinated detective trying to solve a crime no one cares about. Maybe it's that awkward joke you made at the party, the email you sent that you're now *sure* was full of typos, or the fact that you think you waved at someone who didn't wave back—*oh god, they hate you now.*

Sound familiar? That's overthinking, and it's like trying to win a mental game of chess against yourself—you're not going to win, but you'll sure as hell exhaust yourself in the process.

**THE OVERTHINKER'S SPIRAL OF DOOM**

Overthinking is basically your brain's way of going, *Hey, let's take this one minor thing that probably doesn't matter and blow it way the f#ck out of proportion.* And the worst part? Once you start spiraling, it's hard to stop. You go from, *Did I say something weird in that conversation?* to,

*What if they think I'm a total idiot?* to, *I'm probably a terrible person and now I'll die alone surrounded by 17 cats.*

It's mental quicksand. The more you struggle with it, the deeper you sink.

But here's the thing: no one remembers that awkward thing you said. No one's analyzing that email you sent, and I promise you, no one gives a sh#t about your over-the-top greeting or accidental reply-all. People are too busy living in their own heads to obsess over what you're doing. If anything, they've forgotten all about it while *you* are still busy rehashing the whole damn thing.

### WHY WE OVERTHINK

At its core, overthinking is a fear response. You're terrified of doing or saying the "wrong" thing, so your brain replays every possible scenario, hoping to figure out where you messed up or what you could have done differently. It's like you're trying to outsmart embarrassment or avoid rejection by thinking yourself into oblivion.

The problem? You're looking for certainty in situations that are completely out of your control. News flash: You can't control what other people think, and overanalyzing every word you said won't make you any more "perfect." It'll just keep you locked in a loop of self-doubt and mental exhaustion.

**THE PERFECTIONISM CONNECTION**

Overthinking is a cousin of perfectionism—they're both rooted in the need to "get it right." Overthinkers obsess about how they could have done things better, wishing for some unattainable standard of flawless communication, behavior, or decision-making. You're aiming for a version of life where you never make mistakes, never upset anyone, and never look awkward. Guess what? That version of life doesn't exist.

In trying to be perfect, you actually make things worse. Overthinking doesn't solve problems; it creates them. It makes you question your every move and blows tiny things out of proportion. Worst of all, it robs you of peace of mind. You're too busy being mentally tangled up to relax and enjoy the moment.

**HOW TO TURN DOWN THE VOLUME ON OVERTHINKING**

You're not going to eliminate overthinking overnight, but you *can* turn down the volume on the BS loop playing in your head. Here's how to stop obsessing over every little thing and start living a little lighter:

1. **Catch the Spiral Early**
   Overthinking usually starts with a tiny seed of doubt. Maybe you said something awkward, and your brain latches onto it, trying to "fix" it. The trick is catching yourself in the early stages of that spiral. When you notice your thoughts racing, pause. Acknowledge the thought, but don't give it the keys to your brain. You

can think, *Okay, I'm starting to overthink this,* without letting it spiral into a full-blown mental breakdown.

2. **Ask, "Will This Matter in a Week?"**

One of the best ways to snap yourself out of overthinking is to put things in perspective. Ask yourself, *Will this matter in a week? A month? A year?* Chances are, the thing you're obsessing over will be forgotten in a few days (if it even lasts that long). If it's not going to impact your long-term happiness or success, let it go.

3. **Challenge Your Assumptions**

Overthinking is fueled by assumptions, and most of those assumptions are dead wrong. You assume people are judging you, that you made a fool of yourself, or that you've done something unforgivable. But ask yourself—where's the proof? What hard evidence do you have that anyone is still thinking about that comment you made or the way you tripped over your words? Spoiler: there's probably no proof because it's all in your head.

4. **Take Action, Then Let It Go**

Overthinking thrives on inaction. When you're stuck in your head, replaying scenarios over and over, you're not *doing* anything about it. The best way to break the cycle is to take action—send that email, have the conversation, make the decision—then walk the f#ck away. Once you've done your part, there's nothing more to obsess over. Leave it alone and trust that it's enough.

5. **Adopt a "F#ck It" Attitude**

Sometimes the best way to shut down overthinking is to adopt a "f#ck it" mentality. So what if you said something awkward? So what if you didn't nail every detail? Unless you've committed a serious crime (which, if you're reading this, I'm going to assume you haven't), it's probably not that deep. Life's too short to analyze every move you make. Give yourself permission to not care so damn much.

### WHY NO ONE REMEMBERS YOUR F#CK-UPS

Here's the big secret no one tells you: **people don't care as much as you think they do**. Most of us are so wrapped up in our own worlds, we barely register the things other people are doing—let alone store them for future judgment. That awkward thing you said? Yeah, no one's thinking about it because they're too busy worrying about the awkward thing *they* said.

People are self-centered by nature, which is actually a blessing in disguise. It means you have a lot more freedom to mess up without anyone really noticing or caring. Once you accept that no one's keeping a record of your slip-ups, you can stop overanalyzing every little move you make.

### YOUR HOMEWORK: THE OVERTHINKER'S DETOX

This week, I want you to put your overthinking on a diet. Choose one area where you tend to spiral—maybe it's a conversation with a friend, a project at work, or a big decision you're stressing about. The next time you catch yourself overthinking it, stop. Write down the thought that's on repeat in your head, and ask yourself, *Will this matter in a week?* Then, ask yourself, *What action can I take right now to let this go?* Do the thing, and then walk away. No going back, no overanalyzing—just move forward.

If your brain tries to drag you back into the loop, say, *Not today, Satan,* and keep it moving. The goal here isn't to stop overthinking forever (that's impossible), but to break the cycle and get comfortable with letting things go.

**FINAL THOUGHT**

Overthinking is a mental hamster wheel—no matter how fast you run, you're not going anywhere. It's exhausting, pointless, and totally within your power to stop. The next time your brain tries to pull you into an overthinking spiral, remember: no one is paying as much attention to you as you think they are. People are too busy overthinking their own sh#t to worry about yours. So, stop replaying every little thing in your head, take action, and let that sh#t go. Life's too short to spend it stuck in the mental loop of overthinking.

# 7
# PROCRASTINATION

If procrastination was an Olympic sport, you'd be a gold medalist. You've mastered the art of putting things off, whether it's that work project you've been "thinking about starting" or the laundry pile you've somehow managed to avoid for three weeks straight. And when it comes to getting sh#t done? Well, you'll get to it... eventually. Maybe right after you finish scrolling through Instagram for the 47th time today. Sound familiar? Welcome to the club.

Procrastination isn't just about being lazy—it's a f#cked-up coping mechanism. It's what happens when you're trapped between wanting to get things done and being absolutely terrified of getting them wrong. But there's good news: you can break free from this cycle of delay, panic, and guilt. The first step? Understanding why you procrastinate in the first place. Spoiler: It's not because you're lazy. There's more going on under the hood, and it's time to unpack that mess.

## THE REAL REASON YOU PROCRASTINATE

Procrastination is sneaky. On the surface, it looks like laziness or lack of discipline, but that's not it. You're not lying around eating chips all day because you don't care about your goals. In fact, you probably care too much. **Procrastination is rooted in fear.** Fear of failure, fear of judgment, fear of not measuring up. If you put off doing something long enough, you never have to face the possibility that it might not turn out perfectly.

Sound familiar? You're not lazy—you're afraid. You're afraid of diving into the unknown, of putting yourself out there and risking that what you produce might not be "good enough." So instead, you do nothing. Or you do everything *except* the thing you need to do. You clean your room, organize your sock drawer, binge-watch an entire season of that show you've seen three times already—all in the name of avoiding the task that's looming over you. It's classic avoidance behavior, dressed up as "I'll do it later."

## THE PERFECTIONISM-PROCRASTINATION CONNECTION

A lot of procrastination stems from perfectionism. If you can't do something perfectly, why bother doing it at all, right? Wrong. The problem with waiting for the "perfect" time to start is that the perfect time doesn't exist. And here's the kicker: perfectionism makes you believe that your worth is tied to the outcome. If you start that project and it doesn't go well, then maybe you're not as smart, talented, or capable as you thought.

Perfectionism also convinces you that you need to be in the "right" mood, have the "right" tools, or wait for the stars to align before you begin. You tell yourself, *I'll do it when I'm feeling more motivated* or *I'll start when I have more time.* But that magical, mythical "right moment" never comes. So, you push it off and tell yourself you'll get to it later. But spoiler: later never happens.

**THE DOPAMINE HIT OF AVOIDANCE**

Let's be honest—procrastination isn't just fear-based; it's also a bit of a high. Every time you put something off, you get a little dopamine hit. Avoiding the task gives you temporary relief from the anxiety of starting it. You tell yourself, *Ah, I'll deal with it tomorrow,* and for a split second, everything feels lighter. The problem is, that lightness is temporary, and what follows is the crushing weight of guilt and stress as the deadline creeps closer.

Procrastination also tricks you into thinking you work best under pressure. You say things like, *I'll do it when the deadline gets closer; I need that adrenaline rush to focus.* But let's be real—that last-minute panic mode is pure chaos, not productivity. You might get things done, but the quality suffers, and so does your mental health. Waiting until the last minute isn't a superpower; it's a self-sabotage strategy disguised as "working well under pressure."

**HOW TO STOP PROCRASTINATING AND GET SH#T DONE**

Breaking the cycle of procrastination doesn't happen overnight, but it's entirely possible. You don't need more discipline; you need a strategy. Here's how to kick procrastination's ass and start making real progress:

1. **Start Before You're Ready**
   Waiting for the "perfect" moment is a trap. You'll never feel completely ready, so start anyway. The trick is to take the first small step—no matter how minor it is. Write one sentence. Make one phone call. Outline one small part of your project. Once you get the ball rolling, you'll build momentum, and the task won't feel so overwhelming.
2. **Use the 5-Minute Rule**
   Tell yourself you're only going to work on the task for five minutes. That's it. Just five. Once you start, you'll probably keep going because the hardest part is getting started. But even if you only manage five minutes, that's still progress. The goal here is to break through the inertia that keeps you stuck in procrastination mode.
3. **Kill the Perfectionism**
   Aim for progress, not perfection. Done is always better than perfect. Perfectionism makes you procrastinate because you're scared of producing something that's less than ideal. The truth? No one's expecting perfection, except for you. Give yourself permission to suck at first. You can always revise, but you can't revise what you haven't started.
4. **Set Ridiculously Small Goals**
   Procrastination happens when the task feels too big to handle. Break it down into ridiculously small, manageable chunks. Instead of saying, *I need to write a 10-page report,* tell yourself, *I'll write the introduction today.* Tiny goals feel less intimidating and are easier

to tackle. Plus, once you check off that small task, you'll feel a sense of accomplishment, which will motivate you to keep going.
5. **Create Accountability**
Tell someone what you're working on and when you plan to finish it. Knowing someone is expecting results will light a fire under your a##. It could be a friend, a coworker, or even a random post on social media. The point is, once you make it public, you'll feel more committed to getting it done.
6. **Forgive Yourself for Procrastinating**
Beating yourself up for procrastinating only makes it worse. You feel guilty, which leads to more avoidance, which leads to more guilt—a vicious cycle. Instead, forgive yourself for procrastinating in the past and focus on what you can do right now. Every moment is a fresh start. Let go of the guilt and take action.

## WHY PROCRASTINATION ISN'T ALWAYS A BAD THING

Believe it or not, procrastination isn't 100% evil. Sometimes, it's your brain's way of telling you that something isn't quite right. Maybe the task you're avoiding isn't aligned with your goals or values. Or maybe you're procrastinating because you haven't clarified what success looks like for that project. Take a moment to reflect on why you're avoiding certain things. Are you truly procrastinating, or are you hesitating because something about the task feels off? Sometimes, procrastination is just your intuition nudging you to reassess your priorities.

## YOUR HOMEWORK: THE "DO IT NOW" CHALLENGE

For the next week, I want you to tackle one thing you've been procrastinating on—just one. Choose a task that's been hanging over your head and break it down into the smallest possible step. Then, do that step today. Not tomorrow, not later—*right now*. After you've completed that tiny step, celebrate the win. You don't need to finish the entire project in one sitting; you just need to get started.

By the end of the week, reflect on how it felt to take action instead of putting things off. Did the task seem less intimidating once you started? Did the world end because you didn't do it perfectly? (Hint: it didn't.)

### FINAL THOUGHT

Procrastination isn't about being lazy; it's about fear—fear of failure, fear of imperfection, and sometimes fear of success. But here's the truth: the more you put things off, the heavier they become. Every time you procrastinate, you're adding weight to your mental load. The only way to lighten that load is to start—no matter how small. Don't wait for motivation to strike or for the perfect moment to arrive, because spoiler alert: they're not coming. Start now, take action, and watch procrastination lose its grip.

# 8

# FEAR OF SUCCESS

You'd think that success would feel like the ultimate win, right? You work hard, put in the hours, hustle your a## off, and finally achieve your goal. So why the hell does it sometimes feel like a trap? Why, after finally making it, do you feel anxious, stressed, and ready to sabotage the whole damn thing?

Welcome to the bizarre reality of **fear of success**—the mind-f#ck that makes winning feel just as scary as failure. It doesn't make sense on the surface, but this fear runs deep. Success, for all its rewards, can be just as intimidating as falling flat on your face. In fact, sometimes it feels worse because the pressure to *stay* successful creeps in, and suddenly, you're terrified of losing what you've worked so hard to gain. It's the fear that you're not ready, not deserving, or that you'll crumble under the weight of your own achievements.

So, if you've ever found yourself secretly self-sabotaging or avoiding success like it's some kind of punishment, you're not alone. Let's dive into why winning can feel like losing—and how to stop running from the success you've earned.

**WHY WE FEAR SUCCESS**

On the surface, fearing success seems counterintuitive. Success is what we're all striving for, right? But here's the deal: success comes with a whole new set of challenges, responsibilities, and—yep—expectations. And for a lot of people, that's scarier than failure.

1. **Fear of More Pressure**
   Success raises the bar. Once you've "made it," the expectation is that you'll keep achieving at that level—or even higher. Suddenly, you're worried about maintaining your status, reputation, or results. What if you can't keep up? What if you hit your peak and it's all downhill from here? The fear of *not being able to repeat* your success can be paralyzing.
2. **Fear of Losing Relationships**
   Success can be isolating. When you achieve something big, you might notice people around you start acting differently. Maybe they're jealous, or they distance themselves because they feel they don't measure up. On the flip side, you might fear that success will alienate you from your tribe. What if your success causes friction with friends or family? What if people start expecting things from you that you're not ready to give? The fear of losing relationships can hold you back from fully embracing your own success.
3. **Fear of More Visibility**
   With success comes attention—sometimes more at-

tention than you're comfortable with. Suddenly, people are watching you, judging you, and maybe even relying on you. That spotlight can feel suffocating if you're used to flying under the radar. The thought of being seen and scrutinized can be terrifying. What if they realize you're not as great as they think you are?

4.  **Fear of Change**

    Success is a game-changer—literally. Your lifestyle, your schedule, your responsibilities—they all shift when you reach a new level of success. And let's face it, change is scary as hell. Even if the change is positive, it disrupts the comfortable bubble you've been living in. You might fear that success will change you—or worse, that it'll change how people treat you.

**THE SABOTAGE CYCLE**

If you're afraid of success, your brain has a crafty way of sabotaging your progress. Maybe you start procrastinating just when things are going well. Or you play down your achievements, refusing to celebrate because you don't think you deserve the praise. You might even "accidentally" mess up an opportunity because deep down, you're not sure you can handle what comes next.

This is what's called **self-sabotage**—where you actively or subconsciously screw up your own success. You do it to protect yourself from the discomfort of reaching new heights. If you don't succeed, then you don't have to deal with the pressure, the visibility, or the change. It's like you're telling yourself, *It's easier to stay small than to risk falling from the top.*

## REWRITING YOUR STORY: EMBRACING SUCCESS WITHOUT FEAR

So, how do you stop running from success? How do you break the sabotage cycle and actually let yourself *win* without feeling like you're going to implode? Here's how:

1. **Acknowledge the Fear**
   The first step in tackling fear of success is calling it out. Recognize that you're not afraid of failure—you're afraid of what happens *after* success. Name it. Once you see the fear for what it is, you can stop it from sabotaging you.
2. **Redefine Success**
   One of the biggest reasons we fear success is because we've tied it to unrealistic expectations. Redefine what success means for you. It doesn't have to be about perfection or constant growth. Success can mean learning, evolving, and taking things one step at a time. Give yourself permission to succeed *without* the pressure to be flawless or invincible.
3. **Learn to Celebrate**
   When you achieve something, don't brush it off. Own it. Celebrate it. Acknowledge that you've worked hard and you deserve the win. Start small if you need to, but make it a habit to honor your victories—no matter how uncomfortable it feels at first. The more you normalize celebrating success, the less terrifying it becomes.
4. **Focus on the Journey, Not the Outcome**
   Success isn't a one-time thing; it's a journey. Instead of fixating on the end result, shift your focus to the process. What are you learning? How are you grow-

ing? When you stop putting so much weight on the outcome, the fear of maintaining your success starts to fade. You realize that success is about continual effort, not a one-and-done moment.

5. **Prepare for Success**

   Most of us spend so much time preparing for failure that we don't even think about preparing for success. But it's just as important to mentally and emotionally gear up for winning. What will you do when you succeed? How will you handle the changes and pressures that come with it? Having a plan for success makes it feel less overwhelming and more manageable.

6. **Let Go of the Fear of Losing It**

   The fear of success is often rooted in the fear of losing it once you have it. But here's the truth: nothing is permanent. Success will come and go, just like everything else in life. Instead of fearing that you'll lose it, focus on enjoying it while you have it. The pressure to "hold on" to success is what makes it feel like a burden. Let go of that pressure, and you'll be free to enjoy the ride.

**THE HIGH COST OF STAYING SMALL**

Playing small might feel safer, but it comes at a high cost. When you avoid success, you're also avoiding growth, opportunity, and the chance to live your life to the fullest. You're staying in your comfort zone, but you're also staying stuck. And deep down, you know you're capable of more. The only thing standing between you and your next big win is your fear of stepping into the unknown.

Success isn't something to fear—it's something to embrace. Yes, it comes with challenges, but it also comes with incredible rewards. The next time you find yourself running from an opportunity or sabotaging your own success, ask yourself: *Am I playing small because I'm afraid of what happens when I succeed?* If the answer is yes, it's time to flip the script and step into the life you've been working toward.

**YOUR HOMEWORK: THE SUCCESS VISUALIZATION**

This week, I want you to visualize your success—whatever that looks like for you. Imagine yourself achieving your goal, but instead of focusing on the pressure or fear that comes after, focus on the *freedom* it gives you. Picture how success will open doors, create opportunities, and push you to grow. Write down what excites you about succeeding, not what scares you. Use this visualization as a reminder that success is not something to run from—it's something to run toward.

**FINAL THOUGHT**

Fear of success is real, but it's not unbeatable. The more you understand why you're afraid, the more power you have to change the narrative. Success doesn't have to feel like a loss or a trap. It can be a doorway to bigger, better things—if you let it. So, stop running from the pressure, the change, or the expectations. Embrace the fact that you've earned your success, and it's time to step up and own it. Because here's the truth: you're more than ready.

# 9

# COMPARISON TRAP

You're scrolling through Instagram, and boom—there it is. Someone you know just landed the dream job, bought a house with a yard that looks like a Home Depot commercial, or, worse, posted a sun-kissed vacation selfie from some beach in Bali while you're sitting at home, still wearing yesterday's sweatpants. Suddenly, you feel like your life is one big dumpster fire.

Sound familiar? That's the **comparison trap**, and we all fall into it. It's that sneaky little voice in your head that says, *You're not doing enough. You're not enough.* And before you know it, you're drowning in self-doubt, feeling like a loser in the game of life because everyone else seems to be winning. Spoiler alert: **nobody wins at this game.**

The comparison trap is toxic. It's a mental prison where you chain yourself to the impossible task of measuring up to everyone around you. Whether it's your friends, coworkers, or some random stranger with a perfectly curated life on social media, comparison does nothing but steal your joy, waste your energy, and make you feel like you're constantly falling short.

It's time to stop playing this game. Because, in reality, no one's actually winning. Here's why.

**WHY WE COMPARE OURSELVES**

Let's be real: we've been trained to compare ourselves since day one. From school grades to social circles, we've been conditioned to measure our worth by how we stack up against others. It's an ego thing. We look at what others have or what they've achieved and instinctively wonder, *How do I measure up?* The comparison gives us a temporary sense of where we "rank" in life.

And, let's be honest, sometimes comparison feels like sh#t because someone else's success makes us feel inadequate. You're not actually unhappy with your life until you see that someone else is doing "better." But here's the kicker: what you're comparing yourself to is usually an illusion.

Thanks to social media, we now have front-row seats to everyone's highlight reels, but what you don't see are their bloopers. You see the perfect couple photo, but not the argument that happened right before it. You see the promotion announcement, but not the years of hard work, failures, and rejections that led to it. We're comparing our behind-the-scenes to someone else's carefully curated highlight reel—and then wondering why we feel like sh#t.

## THE TRUTH BEHIND THE "PERFECT" LIVES

The truth is, nobody has it all together—not even that influencer who seems to live in a perpetual state of #blessed. Behind every success story, vacation photo, or perfect relationship is a mess of struggles, self-doubt, and screw-ups. But we don't see that part, so we convince ourselves that everyone else is nailing life while we're stumbling around in the dark.

Here's a wild thought: **Everyone's f#cking lost.** Some are just better at faking it. Sure, people may have things you don't, but guess what? You have things they don't. Life isn't about keeping up with others. It's about running your own damn race.

### THE COST OF COMPARISON

The comparison trap does nothing but drain your energy and kill your confidence. It tricks you into focusing on what you *don't* have instead of appreciating what you *do* have. And here's the kicker: the more you compare, the worse you feel. It's a losing game that leaves you mentally exhausted, never satisfied, and always feeling like you're not enough.

There's also a sneaky side effect: comparison breeds resentment. When you're constantly measuring yourself against others, you start resenting them for their success—whether you admit it or not. You feel bitter that they've "made it," and instead of being happy for them, you're low-key pissed that you're not in the same place. But here's the truth: other people's success doesn't take away from yours. There's enough room for everyone to win.

**HOW TO BREAK THE COMPARISON CYCLE**

So, how do you stop playing this f#cked-up game and start focusing on your own damn life? Here's how to escape the comparison trap and take back your mental peace:

1. **Recognize When You're Comparing**
   The first step to breaking the cycle is to catch yourself in the act. The next time you start comparing yourself to someone else—whether it's their career, their relationship, or their shiny new car—hit pause. Ask yourself: *Why am I doing this?* Awareness is the first step to shutting it down.
2. **Celebrate Your Wins**
   Comparison happens when you're focused on what you *don't* have. So flip the script. Take time to celebrate what *you've* achieved. Write it down if you need to—every accomplishment, every milestone, no matter how small. Gratitude for your own journey is the antidote to jealousy of someone else's.
3. **Shift the Focus to Learning**
   Instead of comparing yourself and feeling like sh#t, reframe it as an opportunity to learn. If someone else is where you want to be, ask yourself: *What can I learn from their journey?* Instead of resenting their success, study it. Use it as inspiration for your own path.
4. **Limit Social Media Exposure**
   Social media is like the comparison Olympics—it's a constant stream of curated perfection designed to make you feel like you're falling behind. If scrolling

through your feed leaves you feeling deflated, take a break. Limit your exposure to the highlight reels and spend more time focusing on real life, where things are way messier—and more fulfilling.
5. **Stay in Your Own Lane**
This is the most important one: **run your own race.** You're not competing with anyone but yourself. Life isn't about who gets there first; it's about who enjoys the journey. Your path is yours alone, and it doesn't have to look like anyone else's. The only person you should be comparing yourself to is *who you were yesterday.*

### THE MYTH OF "HAVING IT ALL"

Here's the thing no one tells you: **no one has it all**. The people you're comparing yourself to? They have their own struggles, doubts, and failures—just like you. Sure, they might have things you want, but they're also missing things you have. Everyone's journey is different, and trying to measure your life by someone else's metrics is like comparing apples to oranges. You can't win because the game is rigged.

Stop chasing the illusion of "having it all." That perfect life you're imagining? It doesn't exist. Instead, focus on building a life that *feels* right for you, not one that just *looks* right to others.

### YOUR HOMEWORK: THE COMPARISON DETOX

For the next week, commit to a **comparison detox**. Every time you catch yourself comparing your life to someone else's, pause and flip the script. Instead of thinking, *I wish I had what they have,* replace it with, *I'm grateful for what I have right now.* Write down three things you love about your life every day—things that have nothing to do with anyone else. By the end of the week, you'll realize that your life is pretty damn awesome when you stop measuring it against someone else's.

**FINAL THOUGHT**

The comparison trap is a mental prison where no one wins. It distracts you from your own growth, steals your joy, and makes you feel like you're not enough. But here's the truth: **you are enough**—right now, as you are. Your journey is yours, and it doesn't have to look like anyone else's. So stop comparing your behind-the-scenes to someone else's highlight reel. Life isn't a competition, and the only person you need to impress is yourself. So, let's stop playing this f#cked-up game and start focusing on the only race that matters—*your* race. You vs. you.

# 10

# APPROVAL ADDICTION

Let's talk about validation—the drug you didn't even realize you were addicted to. You know the drill: you post that fire selfie, then obsessively check for likes. You send a text and immediately wonder why they haven't responded. You do something great at work, but instead of basking in your own awesomeness, you wait for someone—*anyone*—to notice and pat you on the back. Sound familiar?

Welcome to **approval addiction**—the exhausting, never-ending chase for external validation. You're constantly looking for someone else to tell you that you're good enough, smart enough, hot enough, or just plain *enough*. And here's the kicker: no matter how much validation you get, it never feels like enough. It's a quick hit of dopamine, but it fades fast, leaving you hungry for more. That's because **approval is a weak a## drug**—it gives you a temporary high, but you always crash afterward, right back into insecurity.

The truth is, seeking validation from others is like chasing a ghost. It doesn't matter how many people tell you you're killing it—if you don't believe it yourself, their approval is like slapping a band-aid on a bullet wound. So, how do we break this habit of chasing approval like it's oxygen? Let's dive into why this addiction is a dead-end and how you can stop living for the applause.

**WHY WE'RE ADDICTED TO APPROVAL**

From the moment we're born, we're hardwired to seek approval. It starts with parents, teachers, and friends, and as we get older, it morphs into needing validation from coworkers, partners, and, let's be honest, random people on the internet. The approval feels good—it gives you a sense of belonging, acceptance, and worthiness. It's like the world is saying, *Hey, you're doing alright!* And who doesn't want to hear that?

But the problem with external validation is that it's a short-term fix for a long-term issue. When you rely on others to tell you you're worthy, you're giving them control over how you feel about yourself. And, surprise, surprise, people are fickle as f#ck. The moment they stop giving you the validation you crave, your self-esteem tanks.

Approval addiction is rooted in fear—the fear that you're not enough on your own. You need someone else to affirm that you matter, that you're successful, that you're lovable. But relying on others for approval is like building your house on quicksand—it'll never hold you up when sh#t gets real.

## THE HIGH OF APPROVAL—AND THE CRASH THAT FOLLOWS

Here's how approval addiction works: You do something that gets noticed—a promotion at work, a killer social media post, or a compliment on your outfit. You feel that rush of validation, like, *Hell yeah, I'm awesome!* But then what? That high wears off. You start questioning whether it was a fluke, and now you're stuck chasing the next fix, the next hit of approval to keep you feeling good about yourself.

The more you chase validation, the more you become dependent on it. You start adjusting your behavior, your choices, and even your personality to get approval. You don't say what you *really* think because you're afraid of offending someone. You don't take risks because you're terrified of being judged. You become a watered-down version of yourself, living for the approval of others instead of your own f#cking happiness.

## WHY APPROVAL IS A SH#TTY CURRENCY

Let's be real: **approval is sh#tty currency**. It's unreliable and unstable. People's opinions change faster than the weather. One minute they're praising you, the next minute they're on to the next shiny thing. If you're constantly living for approval, you're letting other people dictate your value. And here's the thing—most people are too busy dealing with their own insecurities to be your personal validation machine. Chasing approval is a losing game because it puts your self-worth in the hands of people who may not even give a damn about you.

What's worse is that approval can make you feel trapped. Once you start getting it, you feel the pressure to keep up appearances. You become afraid to make mistakes, to fail, or to show vulnerability, because what if people stop approving of you? You end up living your life in a cage, doing things for applause instead of doing them for *you*.

### BREAKING FREE FROM THE APPROVAL TRAP

So, how do you kick the habit of chasing validation like a f#cking junkie? It's not easy, but it's possible. The key is to start building your self-worth from the inside out. Here's how:

1. **Recognize the Patterns**
Start by noticing when you're seeking approval. Do you constantly check for likes or comments? Do you feel anxious when someone doesn't respond the way you wanted? Do you avoid speaking up because you're afraid people won't agree with you? Recognizing the patterns of approval-seeking is the first step to breaking free from them.
2. **Ask Yourself: What Do *I* Think?**
Instead of waiting for someone else to tell you you're awesome, start asking yourself, *What do I think?* Do you like what you did? Do you feel proud of your work, your choices, your actions? If the answer is yes, then that's all the validation you need. You don't need anyone else's permission to feel good about yourself.
3. **Set Boundaries with Social Media**
Social media is a breeding ground for approval addiction. It's designed to make you crave likes, comments,

and shares. Try setting boundaries with how often you check it. Better yet, go on a social media detox. Take a few days—or even a week—off and notice how much lighter you feel when you're not living for the dopamine rush of digital validation.

4. **Do Sh#t for Yourself, Not for Applause**
Stop doing things because you think it'll impress others or get you noticed. Do things because they make *you* happy, proud, and fulfilled. Whether it's a personal project, a new goal, or just how you live your life, make sure you're doing it for *you*. The more you focus on making yourself proud, the less you'll care about what others think.

5. **Learn to Sit with Disapproval**
Here's the uncomfortable truth: you're not going to make everyone happy, and that's okay. Some people are going to disapprove of your choices, your success, or your personality. Let them. Their disapproval has nothing to do with your worth. The more you get comfortable with disapproval, the more you'll realize it's not the end of the world.

**BUILDING INTERNAL VALIDATION**

The real freedom comes when you stop relying on others to validate you and start building that sh#t from the inside. Here's how you can do it:

- **Practice Self-Compassion**: Talk to yourself like you would a friend. When you do something great, acknowledge it. When you make a mistake, don't beat yourself up—learn from it. The more compassion you show yourself, the less you'll need it from others.

- **Create Your Own Metrics for Success**: Decide what success looks like for *you*—not based on what others think, but based on what makes you feel fulfilled. When you live by your own standards, the need for external approval fades.
- **Surround Yourself with People Who Don't Require You to Perform**: Find people who love and accept you for who you are—not for what you can do for them or how "impressive" you seem. When you're around people who don't need you to perform for their approval, you'll feel more free to be yourself.

**YOUR HOMEWORK: THE "F#CK IT, I APPROVE" CHALLENGE**

This week, instead of chasing other people's approval, give yourself permission to be your own biggest fan. Here's how it works: every day, pick one thing you would normally seek validation for—whether it's something you achieved at work, a decision you made, or even how you look. Before you even think about asking someone else for feedback or fishing for compliments, pause. Look yourself in the mirror (literally, if you need to) and say, *F#ck it, I approve.*

Don't just say it—mean it. Own your decision, your success, or even your appearance without needing someone else's stamp of approval. Write it down if that helps: *I approve of _____ because I know it's awesome.*

By the end of the week, you'll have seven moments where you gave yourself the approval you usually look for from others. Reflect on how it feels to take back that power and remind yourself that your opinion is the only one that counts.

**FINAL THOUGHT**

Approval addiction is exhausting and unsustainable. Chasing validation from others is like chasing a high you'll never sustain, and it leaves you feeling empty and dependent. But here's the truth: you don't need anyone's approval to be worthy, valuable, or successful. The only validation that truly matters is your own. So stop living for applause and start living for yourself. Because when you start seeking approval from within, you become f#cking unstoppable.

# PART 2: SOCIAL SURVIVAL

# 11

# SOCIAL ANXIETY

Let's be real—**social anxiety** is like having your brain stuck in panic mode every time you're around people. The sweaty palms, the awkward silences, the mental gymnastics trying to figure out what the hell you're supposed to say next—it's a nightmare. You enter a room full of people and immediately want to melt into the floor. Why? Because your brain is convinced that everyone is watching, judging, and waiting for you to screw up.

Here's the truth: **they're not**. But that doesn't stop social anxiety from making every party, meeting, or casual hangout feel like the Hunger Games of awkwardness. You're just trying to survive, and the idea of thriving in social situations feels about as likely as learning to teleport.

But here's the good news—you don't have to be the life of the party to kill it socially. You don't even have to be comfortable. What you *can* do is learn to not give a sh#t about the things that don't matter, so you can stop overthinking every interaction. So, if the thought of talking to strangers makes you want to curl up in a ball, this chapter's for you. Let's dive into how to stop letting social anxiety run the show.

## WHY SOCIAL ANXIETY FEELS LIKE A DEATH SENTENCE

Social anxiety isn't just about being shy—it's about fearing judgment. You're convinced that the people around you are silently critiquing every word you say, every awkward movement you make, and every stupid joke you attempt. Your brain has you believing that you're under a constant spotlight, and if you make one wrong move, you'll be exiled from society.

It's a survival instinct gone wrong. In ancient times, being part of a tribe was crucial to, you know, *not dying*. So, your brain is wired to fear rejection like it's life or death. Fast forward to today, and now that fear shows up as social anxiety. Your brain thinks that if you say something weird or make a fool of yourself, the tribe (aka, the people around you) will kick you out and leave you to fend for yourself.

Of course, in modern times, no one's actually going to banish you for being awkward. But your brain doesn't know that. So, it sounds the alarms every time you step into a social situation. The result? You freeze, overthink, and spiral into a pit of self-doubt.

## THE "EVERYONE'S WATCHING" ILLUSION

Here's the first big lie social anxiety tells you: *Everyone is watching you.* You walk into a room, and it feels like all eyes are on you, scrutinizing every little thing. But here's the kicker—**people are too busy worrying about**

**themselves to notice you.** Just like you're freaking out about what others think of you, they're doing the same damn thing. Everyone's too wrapped up in their own self-consciousness to care about whether you stuttered or spilled your drink.

Think about it—when was the last time you left a social event and spent hours obsessing over someone else's awkward moment? Exactly. You probably didn't. So why do you think everyone's doing that to you? News flash: **they're not**. Letting go of this "everyone's watching" illusion is the first step to surviving—and thriving—in social situations.

### THE SURVIVAL TOOLKIT FOR SOCIAL ANXIETY

Okay, so now that we know your social anxiety is feeding you a bunch of BS, how do you deal with it? Here's your survival toolkit for handling social situations without feeling like you're going to die inside:

1. **Stop Overthinking Every Word**
   Social anxiety makes you think every word that comes out of your mouth is a potential disaster. But here's the truth: most people aren't dissecting what you say. Small talk isn't about delivering TED Talks—it's about keeping the conversation going. You don't need to be profound, just present. If you stumble over your words or say something awkward, guess what? People will forget it in five minutes (if they even noticed).
2. **Prepare a Few Go-To Questions**
   If small talk makes you want to run for the hills, have a few go-to questions in your back pocket. Peo-

ple love talking about themselves, and asking open-ended questions takes the pressure off you to carry the conversation. Try questions like, *"What's keeping you busy these days?"* or *"What's something you're excited about right now?"* They're broad enough to get people talking, and all you have to do is listen.

3. **Reframe Awkwardness as Relatable**

You think being awkward makes you look bad, but here's the thing—awkwardness is *relatable*. We've all been there. So, instead of seeing your awkward moments as failures, see them as human. The people who matter will appreciate your authenticity. If you make a joke that falls flat or stumble over your words, just laugh it off. You'll be surprised how quickly people move on.

4. **Use the Power of Silence**

Silence feels terrifying when you have social anxiety, but it's not as bad as you think. In fact, silence can make conversations more meaningful. You don't have to fill every gap with words. Take a breath, give people a moment to respond, and don't rush to fill the space. Silence shows that you're comfortable and confident (even if you're faking it).

5. **Stop Playing the Comparison Game**

One of the biggest triggers for social anxiety is comparing yourself to others. You look around and think, *Wow, everyone here is so much more confident, more interesting, more everything.* But guess what? They're not. Confidence doesn't mean you never feel anxious—it just means you don't let anxiety run the show. Stop comparing your insides to someone else's outsides. They're probably struggling just as much as you are.

6. **Set Small, Realistic Goals**
   If the idea of talking to a group of strangers is too overwhelming, break it down. Set small, achievable goals for yourself. Maybe your goal for the night is to have one conversation with someone you don't know, or to stay at the event for at least 30 minutes before deciding if you want to leave. Success isn't about being the most social person in the room; it's about pushing your comfort zone, little by little.
7. **Learn to Be Okay with Discomfort**
   Social anxiety isn't going to magically disappear overnight, but you can learn to manage it by becoming more comfortable with discomfort. Yes, you might feel awkward. Yes, you might say something weird. But that doesn't mean you failed. The goal isn't to eliminate anxiety—it's to get through the moment without letting it control you. The more you expose yourself to uncomfortable situations, the less terrifying they become over time.

**THRIVING INSTEAD OF JUST SURVIVING**

Once you've mastered the art of not giving a sh#t about the small stuff, you'll find that social situations aren't the death traps you imagined. In fact, you might even start to enjoy them. When you stop overanalyzing every interaction, you free yourself up to be more present, more genuine, and—dare I say it—more confident.

Here's the secret: **Confidence isn't about never feeling anxious—it's about moving forward despite the anxiety.** It's about realizing that social situations aren't the end of the world, even if you f#ck up. It's about showing up, doing your best, and letting go of the outcome. When you stop worrying about what people think and start focusing on being present, you'll realize that socializing doesn't have to be a nightmare. It can actually be fun.

### YOUR HOMEWORK: THE "GIVE FEWER F#CKS" EXPERIMENT

This week, I want you to try the **"Give Fewer F#cks" Experiment**. The next time you're in a social situation, set a goal to stop overthinking and just let sh#t happen. Pick one social event (big or small) and tell yourself, *I'm going to give exactly zero f#cks about what people think*. If you say something awkward? Who cares. If there's silence? Let it be. If you feel uncomfortable? Embrace it. Your goal is to survive the moment without letting social anxiety spiral out of control. After the event, reflect on how it went. Did anyone care about your awkwardness as much as you thought they would? (Spoiler: probably not.)

### FINAL THOUGHT

Social anxiety can make you feel like every social interaction is a potential disaster, but here's the reality: **most people aren't thinking about you as much as you think they are**. The key to thriving in social situations isn't becoming the smoothest talker in the room—it's learning to give fewer f#cks about what other people think. So, stop overanalyzing every word, embrace the awkwardness, and remember: no one's watching as closely as you think they are. You've got this—awkward moments and all.

# 12

# FEAR OF REJECTION

Let's face it: **rejection sucks.** Whether it's a job you didn't get, a date that didn't call back, or a project that got shot down, rejection feels like someone just slapped a giant "NOT GOOD ENOUGH" sticker on your forehead. It's that gut punch that leaves you questioning everything about yourself—your worth, your abilities, and whether or not you should just move to a cave and avoid human contact altogether.

But here's the truth about rejection that no one likes to admit: **it's inevitable.** If you're putting yourself out there in any way—whether it's love, work, friendships, or chasing your dreams—rejection is going to happen. Probably a lot. The trick isn't avoiding rejection (because you can't). The trick is learning to not let it break you down into a sad, sh#tty little cookie every time you hear "no."

The truth is, rejection isn't the end of your story—it's a plot twist. It's feedback, not a final sentence. And if you're willing to face it, learn from it, and bounce back stronger, rejection can actually be the thing that pushes you forward. So, let's dive into why rejection isn't as personal as it feels and how to handle it without crumbling into a pile of self-pity.

## WHY REJECTION FEELS LIKE A PERSONAL ATTACK

Rejection hurts because it taps into our deepest fear: *not being enough*. When someone says "no" to you—whether it's a job offer, a relationship, or an idea you pitched—your brain interprets it as, *I'm not good enough. I'm not wanted.* And that sh#t stings. It feels personal, like they're rejecting *you*, not just your proposal, performance, or presence.

But here's the thing—rejection is rarely about you. Most of the time, it's about circumstances, timing, preferences, or someone else's opinion, not about your inherent value. Sure, it feels personal, but it's not a declaration that you suck as a human. Rejection is more about the fit (or lack of fit) than about your worth. It's not a statement on whether you're good enough—it's just a sign that, for this particular thing, at this particular time, it didn't align.

## THE MYTH OF UNIVERSAL ACCEPTANCE

Here's a wild thought: **no one is universally liked, accepted, or successful.** Even the people you look up to—celebrities, leaders, artists, athletes—have faced rejection. Hell, they've probably faced more rejection than you can imagine. The difference is, they didn't let it stop them.

If you're out here trying to get everyone's approval or waiting for a perfect rejection-free life, you're setting yourself up for disappointment. Rejection isn't a sign that you should quit; it's a sign that you're trying. You're pushing boundaries, stepping out of your comfort zone, and putting yourself out there. And that's a hell of a lot better than sitting on the sidelines, terrified of hearing "no."

**WHY REJECTION IS ACTUALLY A GOOD THING**

Wait, what? Rejection is *good*? Yeah, you read that right. Rejection might feel like sh#t in the moment, but it's actually a sign that you're pushing yourself into new territory. You're not playing it safe. You're taking risks, and with risks come rejections.

Think about it—if you never get rejected, you're probably not trying hard enough. You're sticking to the things that are comfortable and guaranteed. But real growth? Real progress? That comes from the moments when you put yourself out there and get knocked down, only to get back up and try again. Rejection builds resilience, and resilience builds success.

**HOW TO BOUNCE BACK FROM REJECTION LIKE A BOSS**

Alright, so rejection is inevitable, and it's not the end of the world. But how do you stop it from wrecking your confidence every time it happens? Here's how to bounce back stronger:

1. **Feel It, but Don't Dwell on It**
   Rejection hurts—let's not sugarcoat that. It's okay to feel the sting, to be disappointed, frustrated, or even pissed off. But don't let it fester. Give yourself a moment to feel it, and then make a conscious decision

to move on. Rejection is just a moment in time—it doesn't have to define your entire mindset.

2. **Detach from the "Personal" Part**
Here's the thing: rejection isn't about your worth as a person. It's about a specific circumstance. Maybe you weren't the right fit for that job, that relationship, or that project—*but that doesn't mean you're not worthy.* Remind yourself that rejection is often about timing, preferences, or other people's baggage. It's not a final judgment on you.

3. **Find the Lesson**
Every rejection holds a lesson—if you're willing to see it. Ask yourself: *What can I learn from this?* Maybe you need to refine your approach, improve your skills, or just wait for a better opportunity. Rejection can be a powerful teacher if you're open to it. Use it as feedback, not failure.

4. **Stop Chasing Universal Approval**
Here's a harsh truth: **not everyone is going to like you or want what you're offering.** And that's okay. Stop chasing the need for universal approval, because it's a game you'll never win. Instead, focus on finding the right people, the right opportunities, and the right fit. When you stop trying to please everyone, rejection stings a lot less.

5. **Keep Putting Yourself Out There**
The worst thing you can do after a rejection is to retreat into your shell and stop trying. Every "no" brings you one step closer to a "yes." The only people who never get rejected are the ones who never take risks. So, keep putting yourself out there. Keep applying for jobs, asking people out, pitching your ideas, and chas-

ing your goals. Rejection might slow you down, but it can't stop you—unless you let it.

6. **Surround Yourself with Support**
When rejection hits hard, it helps to have a solid support system. Talk to people who lift you up, remind you of your strengths, and help you gain perspective. Sometimes all you need is a reminder that you're more than that one "no." Surround yourself with people who believe in you, especially when you don't believe in yourself.

### REJECTION ISN'T THE END—IT'S A REDIRECTION

Rejection isn't a dead-end—it's a detour. It's life's way of pushing you toward something better. Think about all the times you've been rejected in the past. Chances are, you ended up in a better situation because of it. You didn't get that job you wanted, but later found something even more aligned with your goals. You didn't get that relationship you thought you wanted, but dodged a bullet and met someone who truly gets you.

Rejection is a way of clearing the path. It's not the end of your story—it's just one chapter, and it might be the chapter that sets you up for something greater. Don't let rejection stop you; let it fuel you.

### YOUR HOMEWORK: THE "REJECTION CHALLENGE"

This week, I want you to face rejection head-on. Pick something you've been avoiding because you're afraid of hearing "no." Maybe it's applying for that job you're not "qualified" for, asking someone out, pitching a bold idea, or even just trying something new that feels a little scary. The goal isn't to get a "yes"—the goal is to put yourself out there, knowing that rejection is a possibility.

Once you've done it, take note of how you feel. Did the rejection hurt as much as you thought it would? Probably not. By the end of the week, you'll have proof that rejection isn't the end of the world—it's just part of the process. And if you do get a "yes"? Well, that's just a bonus.

**FINAL THOUGHT**

Rejection feels like sh#t in the moment, but it's not a death sentence. It's just a "no" in a world full of potential "yeses." The key to handling rejection is to stop letting it define you. It's not a reflection of your worth—it's just feedback, redirection, or a sign that something better is waiting. So, stop crumbling every time you hear "no," and start seeing rejection for what it really is: a stepping stone to something greater. The only way you truly lose is if you stop trying.

# 13

# LONELINESS

There's nothing quite like that sinking feeling of loneliness. Whether you're scrolling through your phone, staring at a sea of people who seem to have it all—partners, friends, families, thriving social lives—or sitting at home on a Friday night with Netflix asking, *"Are you still watching?"* Yeah, I'm still watching, and apparently still *alone*.

But here's the thing: **loneliness** and **solitude** are not the same f#cking thing. Just because you're alone doesn't mean you have to feel lonely. Society has convinced us that being alone is some kind of failure, like if you're not constantly surrounded by people or in a relationship, something's wrong with you. It's not. In fact, learning to love your alone time is one of the most empowering things you can do for yourself. Solitude doesn't have to feel like a void. It can be your time to thrive—if you stop treating it like a punishment.

So, if you're tired of feeling like the world's forgotten about you or that your phone is allergic to receiving texts, it's time to change the narrative. Let's dive into why we feel lonely, how to embrace being alone without crumbling, and how to stop thinking that being alone means you're destined to die surrounded by cats (though, honestly, there are worse ways to go).

### WHY LONELINESS FEELS LIKE SH#T

Loneliness isn't just about being physically alone—it's the emotional weight of feeling disconnected. You can be in a room full of people and still feel like you're stranded on your own personal deserted island. That's because loneliness isn't about *who's around you*; it's about *how connected you feel* to them. It's that gut punch of feeling unseen, unheard, and unloved.

This hits hard in a world that constantly bombards us with images of people who *seem* to have it all—perfect relationships, endless friend groups, family dinners that look like a Hallmark movie set. It's easy to feel like you're on the outside looking in, like you're missing out on some secret party everyone else was invited to.

But here's the truth: **being alone doesn't mean you're unloved, and being surrounded by people doesn't mean you're fulfilled**. It's about connection, yes, but it's also about the story you tell yourself about being alone. You've been trained to believe that solitude is failure—that if you're not constantly busy with plans, people, or a partner, you're somehow lacking. That's bullsh#t.

### THE DIFFERENCE BETWEEN LONELINESS AND SOLITUDE

The real problem isn't being alone—it's what you think being alone means. Loneliness is the feeling of isolation, the sense that you're unwanted or left out. Solitude, on the other hand, is the art of being alone without being lonely. It's a space where you can recharge, reflect, and reconnect with yourself. Solitude is powerful, but loneliness convinces you it's tragic.

Here's the trick: **when you own your alone time, you stop being a victim of loneliness.** You start seeing your time by yourself as an opportunity for growth, self-discovery, and, hell, even fun. You're not "alone" in the sad, forgotten sense—you're simply choosing to enjoy your own company. There's a massive difference.

### THE TRAP OF CONSTANT COMPARISON

Part of why loneliness feels so soul-crushing is because we're constantly comparing ourselves to the highlight reels of others. You see your friend's Instagram story of them at brunch with their squad and immediately feel like a loser because you spent the day binge-watching TV and eating cereal for dinner. But here's the kicker: **you're comparing your reality to their curated content**. You don't see the parts of their day when they, too, felt alone or insecure. Everyone's dealing with sh#t—you just don't see it in their filtered selfies.

Comparison is a toxic habit that turns solitude into a shame spiral. The more you scroll and compare, the more you convince yourself that you're not "enough" because you're alone. But news flash: **other people's lives are not your measuring stick**. Your worth isn't determined by how full your social calendar is.

## HOW TO OWN YOUR ALONE TIME

Now that we've debunked the myth that being alone is some kind of failure, let's talk about how to embrace solitude like the boss you are. Here's how to turn loneliness into empowerment and thrive in your own company:

1. **Shift the Narrative**
   Stop treating being alone as a punishment. Instead, think of it as a f#cking opportunity. This is your time—your chance to do whatever the hell you want without answering to anyone else. No one's judging you for binge-watching reality TV, for spending three hours deep-diving into weird YouTube documentaries, or for experimenting with that random hobby. Your alone time is your time to do *you*.
2. **Stop Waiting for Someone Else to Fill the Void**
   One of the biggest traps of loneliness is thinking that someone else—whether it's a friend, a partner, or even a stranger—will come along and make you feel less alone. But here's the reality: **no one can complete you**. You are not an incomplete puzzle waiting for someone else to fill in the missing pieces. The key to overcoming loneliness is learning to feel whole on your own. That doesn't mean you don't want connections, but it means you don't rely on them for your sense of self.
3. **Find Solitude Activities That Recharge You**
   Just because you're alone doesn't mean you have to sit in silence feeling sorry for yourself. Find activities that make solitude feel like a treat instead of a burden. That could be anything from reading, writing,

drawing, cooking, going for a walk, or even treating yourself to a solo movie or dinner. Yes, **you can go to a restaurant alone without looking like a weirdo**. Trust me, no one's watching.

4. **Reframe Loneliness as a Phase, Not a Forever**
When loneliness hits, it can feel like it's going to last forever, like you're doomed to live a solitary life forevermore. But here's the truth: loneliness is a **temporary** feeling, not a permanent state of being. Remind yourself that this is just a season—like any emotion, it will pass. And when you stop fearing loneliness, it loses its power over you.

5. **Strengthen Your Relationship with Yourself**
The real benefit of spending time alone is that you get to know yourself on a deeper level. You start understanding your own needs, thoughts, and feelings in a way that's hard to do when you're constantly surrounded by others. Use your alone time to reconnect with yourself—what do you *really* want? What makes you happy when no one's around to see? When you build a stronger relationship with yourself, solitude becomes empowering instead of isolating.

**WHY YOU'RE NEVER REALLY "ALONE"**

Here's something you need to remember: **you're never truly alone.** Even in your quietest, most isolated moments, you're part of something bigger. Whether it's your community, your family, your circle of friends, or just the human experience, you're connected. Feeling lonely doesn't mean you're *actually* alone—it just means you're craving connection. And guess what? Connection comes in many forms, not just the physical presence of others.

Sometimes, all you need to do to shake that lonely feeling is to reach out—send a text, make a phone call, connect with someone who matters. And sometimes, it's about realizing that you can be your own best company.

### YOUR HOMEWORK: THE SOLITUDE EXPERIMENT

This week, I want you to take the **Solitude Experiment**. Set aside one day to intentionally spend time alone—but instead of seeing it as a sad, lonely day, reframe it as a day to enjoy your own company. Pick an activity you've been meaning to do (whether it's something creative, relaxing, or just fun) and do it solo. No phones, no distractions, no reaching out for validation—just you.

By the end of the day, reflect on how it felt to spend intentional time with yourself. Did it feel empowering? Awkward? Relaxing? The goal here is to get comfortable with your own company, to realize that being alone doesn't mean being lonely—it just means you're enjoying the luxury of being with the only person who will always have your back: *you*.

### FINAL THOUGHT

Loneliness can feel like a heavy burden, but it's not your enemy. It's a sign that you're craving connection—not just with others, but with yourself. When you learn to own your alone time and stop confusing solitude with loneliness, you take back your power. You stop waiting for someone else to make you feel whole and start realizing that you're already complete on your own. So, if you've been feeling like the world's forgotten about you, think again—*you* haven't forgotten about you. And that's the only connection you need to thrive.

# 14

# BEING TOO MUCH OR NOT ENOUGH

You know that feeling, right? The nagging suspicion that you're either *too much*—too loud, too bold, too opinionated—or *not enough*—not smart enough, not attractive enough, not interesting enough. It's like no matter what you do, you're constantly walking a tightrope between "trying too hard" and "not trying hard enough."

Welcome to the exhausting mental f#ckery of wondering if you're ever the right amount of *anything* for anyone. But here's the truth: **you are exactly the right amount of f#cking awesome, just as you are**. The problem isn't that you're too much or not enough—it's that you've been measuring yourself by everyone else's standards. And spoiler alert: those standards are impossible, inconsistent, and frankly, bullsh#t.

In this chapter, we're diving deep into the fear that you're never quite "right" for the world around you, how to stop bending yourself into shapes that don't fit, and how to own who the hell you are—without apology.

## THE "TOO MUCH" VS. "NOT ENOUGH" MINDF#CK

So, what is this fear of being too much or not enough? It's that constant internal debate where no matter what you do, it feels like you're coming up short. Speak your mind? *You're too much.* Stay quiet? *You're not enough.* Go after what you want? *You're too ambitious.* Take a backseat? *You're not trying hard enough.*

The kicker is, these feelings often come from conflicting messages we've absorbed over time—from society, from family, from past relationships. You've been told, directly or indirectly, to dial down certain parts of yourself while amplifying others. You're supposed to be confident but not cocky, ambitious but not pushy, kind but not a doormat, assertive but not aggressive. It's like you're constantly getting contradictory memos on how to "be," and frankly, it's exhausting.

### WHY YOU FEEL "TOO MUCH" OR "NOT ENOUGH"

At its core, this fear comes from a deep-seated need for acceptance. You want to belong, to be liked, to be loved. But the problem with tying your worth to how others perceive you is that you'll never hit the sweet spot—because it doesn't exist. No matter what you do, someone, somewhere, is going to think you're *too much* of this or *not enough* of that.

The truth is, **being "too much" or "not enough" is a reflection of someone else's comfort level, not your value**. When someone says you're too much, what they're really saying is, *I can't handle this part of you.* When someone implies you're not enough, they're projecting their own insecurities onto you. It's not your job to shrink yourself to fit their version of "just right."

## THE TRAP OF PEOPLE-PLEASING

Part of the reason this "too much" vs. "not enough" mind game gets so deeply ingrained is because of people-pleasing. You've spent so much time trying to mold yourself into whatever version of "you" that you think people want. You've silenced yourself when you felt too loud, toned down your ambition when you felt too driven, and hid your quirks when you thought they were too weird.

But here's the thing: **you're never going to please everyone**. No matter how much you twist and contort yourself to fit someone else's standards, you'll still be "too much" for some and "not enough" for others. So why the hell are you wasting your energy? People-pleasing is a losing game. The only person you need to please is *yourself*.

## YOU'RE THE RIGHT AMOUNT, PERIOD.

Now, let's get one thing straight: **you are not "too much" or "not enough"—you're the right amount of awesome, just as you are**. The problem isn't that you need to change who you are; the problem is that you've been told you need to fit into these arbitrary boxes of acceptability. But f#ck the boxes. You don't exist to make other people comfortable. You exist to be your fullest, most authentic self—flaws, quirks, and all.

The people who matter will love you for exactly who you are, not for the version of you that's been watered down or stretched thin. You don't need to dim your light because it's too bright for someone else. And you sure as hell don't need to add more sparkle just to fit someone's standards.

**HOW TO OWN YOUR "TOO MUCH" OR "NOT ENOUGH"**

So, how do you stop this back-and-forth mental torment and start owning who you are? Here's how to embrace your fullness—without apology:

1. **Recognize the BS Standards**
   The first step to breaking free from this trap is recognizing that most of the standards you're trying to live up to are total BS. Society is always going to have conflicting expectations of you: Be bold, but not too bold. Be independent, but not so independent that you intimidate people. Screw that. Realize that there is no universal standard for how you should be. The only standard that matters is yours.
2. **Stop Apologizing for Who You Are**
   If you've spent years apologizing for being "too much" or "not enough," it's time to stop. Own the parts of yourself that you've been told are too loud, too bold, or too weird. Those are probably the most interesting parts of you. And if someone can't handle it? They're not your people. You don't need to shrink yourself to fit into someone else's comfort zone.
3. **Embrace Your "Too Much" as a Superpower**
   The things you've been told to tone down—your passion, your drive, your honesty? Those are your superpowers. You're not "too much"—you're *powerful*, and

not everyone knows how to handle that. But that's their problem, not yours. What's seen as "too much" in one context can be a game-changer in another. Own your power.

4. **Redefine "Enough" for Yourself**
You are enough, right now, as you are. The trick is realizing that "enough" doesn't have to come from external validation. You don't need to be prettier, smarter, funnier, or more "put together" to deserve respect, love, and success. You're enough simply because you exist. You get to define what "enough" means—not society, not your parents, not your friends.

5. **Set Boundaries Like a Boss**
If someone makes you feel like you're "too much" or "not enough," it's time to set some boundaries. You don't have to shrink yourself to make others comfortable. Boundaries aren't about shutting people out—they're about protecting your energy and refusing to mold yourself to fit into someone else's expectations. If people can't handle the full version of you, they don't get access to you.

**THE FEAR OF BEING "TOO MUCH" IN RELATIONSHIPS**

This fear of being too much or not enough hits hardest in relationships. You worry that if you show your full self—your intensity, your quirks, your needs—you'll scare people off. So, you tone it down, hoping that if you make yourself smaller, you'll be more lovable. But here's the deal: **the right people will love you for exactly who you are**. The wrong people? They'll always find a reason to make you feel like you're too much or not enough.

Stop dating or being friends with people who make you feel like you're hard to love. You're not difficult, and you don't need to change who you are to fit into someone else's box. The right people will stick around not *despite* your fullness, but *because* of it.

**YOUR HOMEWORK: THE "TOO MUCH, NOT ENOUGH" CHALLENGE**

This week, I want you to identify one area of your life where you've been holding back because you're afraid of being "too much" or "not enough." Maybe it's a part of your personality that you've toned down, a passion you've been keeping under wraps, or a conversation you've avoided because you didn't want to seem overbearing.

Now, here's your challenge: **stop holding back.** Show up fully. Be "too much" if you have to. Speak your mind, embrace your quirks, and refuse to apologize for taking up space. By the end of the week, reflect on how it felt to let go of the fear of being "too much" or "not enough." Did the world end? Did people freak out? Probably not. And even if they did—*f#ck 'em*. You're not here to live life for anyone else's comfort.

**FINAL THOUGHT**

You've spent enough time worrying about being too much or not enough. It's time to recognize that you're exactly the right amount of awesome, just as you are. You don't need to shrink, dim, or dilute yourself to fit into anyone else's narrow definition of "acceptable." The people who matter will love you for your fullness, and the ones who don't can get lost. So, stop the mental back-and-forth and start living unapologetically as the bold, brilliant, and beautifully messy human you are. Because, spoiler alert: *

# 15

# BODY IMAGE

Let's be real—**body image issues** suck. Whether it's standing in front of a mirror, scrolling through your social media feed, or just walking down the street, it's easy to feel like you're not measuring up. Maybe it's your weight, your height, your skin, or even the shape of your nose. We all have that *one thing* (or, let's be honest, a long list of things) we're convinced is "wrong" with us.

But here's the kicker: **your body isn't the problem—your mindset is.** The real issue is the warped, bullsh#t lens through which you view yourself, shaped by years of toxic messaging from society, media, and, sometimes, the people around you. The diet industry, fashion world, and social media influencers have been selling you the same lie for years: *If you just looked like this—if you were thinner, taller, curvier, more toned—then you'd be happy, loved, and successful.* Spoiler alert: it's a load of f#cking garbage.

Your body isn't the problem. It never was. The problem is the way you've been trained to view yourself—as something to be fixed, perfected, and constantly scrutinized. It's time to break down that distorted mindset and start learning how to love the skin you're in, not in some cheesy, "just be positive!" way, but in a real, practical, and unapologetic way.

## THE WARPED LENS OF SELF-PERCEPTION

Body image issues don't come out of nowhere. From a young age, we're bombarded with messages about how we *should* look. Magazines, TV, Instagram, TikTok—everywhere you look, there's a narrow, unattainable standard of beauty being shoved down your throat. And the worst part? You start to believe it. You start thinking that if you don't look like that model, influencer, or celebrity, you're not good enough. You start picking apart your reflection, noticing every "flaw" and convincing yourself that those flaws are what's holding you back from happiness or success.

But here's the truth: **the problem isn't your body—it's the impossible standards you're comparing yourself to.** You're trying to measure up to airbrushed, edited, and filtered images that don't reflect real life. And the more you try to change your body to fit that mold, the more disconnected you become from who you truly are.

The issue is your **perception**—not your reflection. You've been looking at yourself through a distorted lens, shaped by years of societal conditioning. And it's time to smash that lens and see yourself for who you really are.

## THE MYTH OF THE "PERFECT" BODY

Let's get one thing straight: **the "perfect" body doesn't exist.** That idealized version of a body you've been chasing? It's a moving target that's always out of reach. Why? Because beauty standards change all the f#cking time. What's considered "beautiful" today might not have been considered beautiful 50 years ago, and it might not be in another 50.

And here's the kicker: **no one looks perfect all the time**. Not even the people you idolize on social media. Those carefully curated posts you see are the result of strategic lighting, poses, filters, and, often, a little Photoshop magic. The influencers and models you compare yourself to? They don't even look like that in real life. It's all an illusion. So why the hell are you measuring yourself against something that isn't even real?

The idea of a "perfect body" is a myth designed to keep you feeling insecure and spending money on diet programs, beauty products, and fitness fads. It's time to stop playing that game. Perfection isn't real, and it sure as hell isn't necessary.

## HOW TO START LOVING THE SKIN YOU'RE IN

So, how do you break free from the toxic cycle of body shaming yourself and start embracing your body for the incredible thing it is? It's not about pretending to love every inch of yourself 24/7—that's not realistic. It's about learning to appreciate, respect, and ultimately, accept your body without constantly trying to change it. Here's how:

1. **Challenge Your Negative Thoughts**

    Every time you catch yourself thinking something sh#tty about your body, pause and ask yourself, *Where is this thought coming from?* Is it your thought, or is it a message you've absorbed from years of toxic beauty standards? Chances are, it's the latter. Once you identify the source of the thought, you can start to dismantle it. Replace it with something kinder, even if it's as simple as, *My body is fine the way it is.*

2. **Stop the Comparison Game**

    The quickest way to feel like sh#t about your body is to compare it to others. Remember, everyone's body is different. There's no one-size-fits-all when it comes to beauty. Instead of focusing on what your body isn't, start appreciating what it is. Maybe your legs aren't as long as that model's, but they carry you through every day, and that's pretty damn powerful. Shift your focus to what your body can *do*, not what it *looks like* compared to someone else.

3. **Practice Body Neutrality**

    You don't have to love your body every day, but you can respect it. **Body neutrality** is about taking the focus off your appearance and putting it on how you feel. Your body is the vessel that gets you through life. It carries you, protects you, heals you, and sustains you. It doesn't have to be "perfect" to be worthy of respect and care. Start by treating your body with kindness—feed it, move it, rest it—not to fit some aesthetic goal, but because it deserves it.

4. **Diversify Your Social Media Feed**

    If your Instagram feed is full of picture-perfect influencers, it's time for a detox. Start following people who show real, diverse bodies—bodies of all shapes, sizes, and abilities. Seeing a broader range of body types can help shift your perspective and remind you that beauty comes in many forms, not just the airbrushed ones.

5. **Speak Kindly to Yourself**
The way you talk to yourself about your body matters. If you're constantly criticizing, belittling, or insulting yourself, it's no wonder you feel like sh#t. Start changing the conversation in your head. Instead of looking in the mirror and immediately pointing out what you hate, try pointing out something you appreciate. It could be as simple as, *My arms are strong* or *My skin feels soft today*. It might feel weird at first, but over time, these small shifts will add up.

6. **Surround Yourself with Body-Positive People**
The people you surround yourself with can influence how you feel about your body. If you're constantly around people who talk about dieting, body shaming, or "fixing" themselves, it's easy to get sucked into that mindset. Find friends who support body positivity, who aren't obsessed with the superficial, and who appreciate you for who you are, not what you look like.

**YOUR BODY IS NOT THE ENEMY—IT'S YOUR HOME**

Here's the thing: **your body isn't the enemy.** It's your home. It's what allows you to experience life, to laugh, to move, to love, to create. It's where you live. And it deserves your love and respect—not because it's perfect, but because it's *yours*. You only get one body in this life, so why spend all your time and energy hating it?

Loving your body doesn't mean you have to love every part of it all the time, but it does mean accepting it as it is—right now, without conditions. Your worth isn't determined by your appearance. You are enough, exactly as you are, in the body you have today.

**YOUR HOMEWORK: THE MIRROR CHALLENGE**

This week, I want you to stand in front of a mirror every day and pick one thing about your body that you appreciate. It doesn't have to be something you love, just something you can appreciate. Maybe it's your strong legs, your hands that let you create, or even just your eyes that let you see the world. Say it out loud. **Every. Single. Day.** The goal isn't to fake love for your body overnight—it's to start shifting your mindset from criticism to appreciation.

By the end of the week, notice how you feel. Has your perception of your body shifted, even a little? Keep practicing this habit, and over time, you'll start to build a healthier, more positive relationship with the skin you're in.

**FINAL THOUGHT**

Your body isn't the problem—your mindset is. It's time to break free from the toxic cycle of body shaming and start appreciating yourself for who you are, not who you think you *should* be. You don't need to look like a model, an influencer, or anyone else to be worthy of love, success, and happiness. You are already enough, in the body you have, right now. It's time to stop hating your reflection and start embracing the fact that your body is f#cking awesome—because it's yours.

# 16

# FEAR OF INTIMACY

You've met someone great. Things are going well. You're vibing, connecting, and feeling closer than you've ever felt with anyone. But then, out of nowhere, **you start freaking the f#ck out**. Suddenly, you're pulling back, overanalyzing everything, picking fights, or finding reasons why it won't work. The walls go up, and before you know it, you're back to pushing that person away—again. Sound familiar?

This is what happens when you're dealing with the **fear of intimacy**. It's that deep-rooted fear of letting someone get too close, of being vulnerable, of opening up and possibly getting hurt. On the surface, you might think you want love, connection, and closeness, but when it starts to happen, your fear hijacks your brain and pushes you into full-on sabotage mode. You're scared that if you let someone in, they'll see the real you, flaws and all, and maybe, just maybe, they won't like what they find. So, you push them away before they can reject you.

But here's the thing: **intimacy is terrifying because it requires real vulnerability**—letting someone see the messy, imperfect, human parts of you. The parts you usually try to hide. If the thought of letting someone in close scares the sh#t out of you, you're not alone. But the fear of intimacy isn't something you have to live with forever. You can stop sabotaging your relationships and start building real, meaningful connections. Let's break down why getting close feels like a threat and how to stop pushing people away.

### WHY INTIMACY FEELS SO SCARY

Intimacy—whether it's emotional, physical, or both—requires trust, openness, and vulnerability. And that's where things get tricky. **Vulnerability** means showing up as your true self, with all your baggage, fears, and imperfections laid bare. It means letting someone see you fully, without the mask you usually wear to protect yourself. And that's f#cking terrifying.

Why? Because if someone rejects the real you, it feels like a deeper kind of hurt. If they reject the polished, guarded version of you, fine—you weren't showing them the whole truth anyway. But if you let them in close, and they reject you? That's a whole different level of pain. So, to avoid that potential heartbreak, you keep people at arm's length. It's a defense mechanism, a way to protect yourself from being hurt. But in doing so, you're also keeping yourself from experiencing the real connection you crave.

### THE CYCLE OF PUSHING PEOPLE AWAY

Here's how the fear of intimacy usually plays out:

1. **You meet someone** who seems like they could be a great partner or friend. You start to feel connected, and it feels good—at first.
2. **Things start getting real**. The relationship deepens, and suddenly, you're not just sharing surface-level stuff anymore. You're starting to open up, be vulnerable, and let them in.
3. **Your fear kicks in**. The closer you get, the more anxious you feel. You start overthinking, wondering if you're too much or not enough. You fear they'll see the "real" you and leave.
4. **You sabotage**. To protect yourself, you push them away. Maybe you start picking fights, creating distance, or convincing yourself that they don't care about you as much as you care about them.
5. **The relationship ends**. You've successfully avoided the risk of intimacy, but now you're alone again, wondering why things never seem to work out.

And then the cycle repeats.

### THE ROOTS OF INTIMACY FEAR: WHY YOU KEEP RUNNING

Your fear of intimacy didn't come out of nowhere. It's likely rooted in past experiences—whether it's a bad breakup, rejection, or emotional wounds from childhood. Maybe you learned early on that getting close to people meant getting hurt. Maybe someone you trusted betrayed you, or maybe you grew up in an environment where vulnerability wasn't safe.

Whatever the reason, your brain has learned that closeness equals danger. So, every time you start getting close to someone, your mind goes into survival mode, throwing up emotional walls to protect you from getting hurt again. But here's the problem: those walls don't just keep out pain—they keep out love, connection, and intimacy, too.

**HOW TO STOP SABOTAGING YOUR RELATIONSHIPS**

If you're tired of pushing people away and feeling alone because of it, it's time to start breaking down those walls. Here's how to stop sabotaging your relationships and start embracing intimacy—without losing your sh#t:

1. **Acknowledge Your Fear**
   The first step to overcoming your fear of intimacy is recognizing that it's there. Be honest with yourself: when things start getting real, do you pull back? Do you find yourself looking for reasons to bail when a relationship gets close? Acknowledge the pattern and realize that your fear of getting hurt is driving your behavior.
2. **Challenge Your Beliefs**
   Fear of intimacy often comes from deeply ingrained beliefs, like *"If they see the real me, they won't love me"* or *"I'll get hurt if I get too close."* But here's the thing: those beliefs aren't facts. They're assumptions based on past experiences, and they're holding you back. Start challenging them. Ask yourself: *Is it true that getting close will always end in pain?* What if the opposite is true—what if getting close could lead to something beautiful?

3. **Take Small Steps Toward Vulnerability**

   You don't have to tear down your emotional walls all at once. Start small. Practice being vulnerable in low-stakes situations—share something personal with a friend, express your feelings more openly, or let yourself be seen in a moment of imperfection. The more you practice vulnerability, the less terrifying it becomes. Intimacy is built one small, honest moment at a time.

4. **Communicate Your Fears**

   If you're in a relationship (or getting close to someone), be honest about your fear of intimacy. Let them know that getting close feels scary for you and that sometimes, you might need patience as you work through it. The right person will appreciate your honesty and won't run away just because you're afraid. In fact, being open about your fears can bring you closer.

5. **Reframe Vulnerability as Strength**

   We've been taught to think of vulnerability as weakness, but the truth is, **vulnerability is a sign of strength**. It takes courage to let someone see the real you, to risk being hurt, and to show up fully in a relationship. Vulnerability isn't about being "weak"—it's about being real. And real connection only happens when you let go of the fear of being hurt and embrace the possibility of being seen.

6. **Be Patient with Yourself**

   Fear of intimacy doesn't disappear overnight. It's a process, and it takes time to unlearn the patterns that have kept you from getting close. Be patient with yourself, and don't expect perfection. You're going to slip up sometimes, and that's okay. The goal isn't to be fearless—it's to stop letting your fear control you.

### WHY LETTING PEOPLE IN IS WORTH THE RISK

Here's the truth: **intimacy is always a risk.** There's no guarantee that getting close to someone won't result in pain. People are messy, relationships are complicated, and sometimes things don't work out. But if you're constantly running from the possibility of getting hurt, you're also running from the possibility of real love, connection, and belonging.

At the end of the day, pushing people away doesn't protect you—it isolates you. Yes, letting people in is scary as hell, but it's also the only way to build the deep, meaningful relationships you want. The risk of getting hurt is worth it because the reward—true connection—is life-changing.

### YOUR HOMEWORK: THE "LOWER THE WALL" EXPERIMENT

This week, instead of diving straight into vulnerability, try the **"Lower the Wall" Experiment**. The next time you feel yourself pulling back in a relationship—whether it's avoiding a deep conversation, deflecting a compliment, or shutting down emotionally—*pause*. Ask yourself, *Am I pushing this person away because I'm scared of getting too close?* If the answer is yes, **take a small step toward openness**.

It could be as simple as allowing the conversation to go deeper instead of changing the subject, sharing a personal story, or even just staying emotionally present when you feel tempted to distance yourself. Afterward, reflect on how it felt to "lower the wall" a little. Did anything bad happen? Were you more connected than you thought possible?

This experiment is all about taking tiny steps toward intimacy without overwhelming yourself. Each time you lower the wall, you'll start to see that vulnerability is less scary—and more rewarding—than you've been telling yourself.

**FINAL THOUGHT**

Fear of intimacy is a defense mechanism—one that's trying to protect you from being hurt. But the walls you've built to keep out pain are also keeping out love, connection, and everything that makes relationships meaningful. It's time to stop sabotaging your connections and start letting people in. Yes, intimacy is scary, and yes, there's a chance you might get hurt—but there's also a chance you'll find the deep, real connection you've been craving. And that's a risk worth taking.

# 17

# PEOPLE-PLEASING

Let's get straight to it: **people-pleasing is exhausting.** You're constantly bending over backward to make sure everyone else is happy, comfortable, and taken care of—meanwhile, you're left feeling drained, unappreciated, and straight-up pissed off. But saying "no"? That feels impossible. You're convinced that if you stop saying yes to every request, every favor, and every last-minute "help me out" plea, people will think you're selfish or, worse, a complete a##hole.

But here's the harsh truth: **people-pleasing doesn't make people like you more—it just makes you a doormat.** When you're constantly putting others' needs ahead of your own, you end up losing yourself in the process. And the more you say "yes" to things you don't want to do, the more resentment builds up inside you, making you bitter and burnt out.

It's time to break the people-pleasing cycle. It's time to stop giving so many f#cks about what other people think and start prioritizing your own damn needs. This chapter is all about learning to say "no" without feeling guilty, setting boundaries like a pro, and reclaiming your energy, your time, and your self-worth.

**WHY YOU'RE STUCK IN THE PEOPLE-PLEASING TRAP**

People-pleasing comes from a good place—it's rooted in the desire to be liked, to avoid conflict, and to keep the peace. Maybe you were raised to always be "nice," or maybe you learned early on that the easiest way to avoid rejection or disapproval was to say "yes" to everything. You've convinced yourself that the more agreeable you are, the more people will love and accept you.

But here's the problem: **people-pleasing isn't about kindness—it's about fear.** You're not saying "yes" because you genuinely want to help; you're saying "yes" because you're scared of what will happen if you say "no." You're afraid people will be mad, disappointed, or think less of you. You're terrified of rocking the boat, so you keep sacrificing your own needs to keep everyone else happy.

The result? You end up feeling resentful, overworked, and invisible. People start expecting you to be there at their beck and call because you've trained them to expect that from you. And worse, you lose sight of your own needs because you're too busy living for everyone else.

**WHY SAYING "NO" FEELS SO F#CKING HARD**

Saying "no" feels hard for two big reasons:

1. **You're Afraid of Conflict**
    You've spent your life avoiding conflict like it's the plague. You're terrified that if you say "no," it will lead to an argument, hurt feelings, or someone being mad

at you. And because conflict makes you uncomfortable, you'd rather say "yes" and avoid the awkwardness altogether.
2. **You Tie Your Self-Worth to Being Liked**
Deep down, you believe that your worth is tied to how much you do for others. If you're not the helpful, agreeable person everyone can count on, what value do you have? This belief is what keeps you stuck in the people-pleasing cycle—you think you have to keep saying "yes" to prove your value, even if it means sacrificing your own happiness.

But here's the thing: **saying "no" doesn't make you a bad person**. In fact, saying "no" is one of the most powerful things you can do to protect your energy, your time, and your mental health. You're not responsible for everyone else's happiness, and you don't owe anyone an explanation for prioritizing your own well-being.

### HOW TO STOP BEING A DOORMAT

If you're ready to break free from people-pleasing and start reclaiming your time and energy, here's how to do it:

1. **Start Small**
If you've been a lifelong people-pleaser, saying "no" right off the bat might feel impossible. So, start small. Practice saying "no" in low-stakes situations. Maybe it's turning down an invite to an event you don't really want to attend or saying no to a small favor that feels more like an obligation. The more you practice, the easier it gets.

2. **Get Comfortable with Discomfort**

   Here's the truth: saying "no" will feel uncomfortable at first. You'll probably worry that you're disappointing people or that they're going to think less of you. That's normal. But discomfort doesn't mean you're doing something wrong—it means you're breaking a habit. Over time, you'll learn that the world doesn't fall apart when you say "no." In fact, people will start respecting your boundaries more.

3. **Stop Over-Explaining**

   When you finally muster up the courage to say "no," you might feel the urge to explain yourself, justify your decision, or give a list of reasons why you can't say yes. Don't. **"No" is a complete sentence.** You don't owe anyone an explanation for why you're prioritizing your own needs. Simply say, *"I'm not able to do that,"* and leave it at that. The less you over-explain, the more confident you'll feel.

4. **Set Boundaries and Stick to Them**

   People-pleasers often have weak or non-existent boundaries. It's time to start setting some. Boundaries are not about keeping people out; they're about protecting your energy and well-being. Whether it's limiting how much time you spend helping others or deciding that you're no longer available for last-minute favors, boundaries are essential. And once you set them, **stick to them**. People might push back at first, but eventually, they'll get used to the new you.

5. **Accept That Not Everyone Will Like You**

   Here's the hard truth: **not everyone is going to like you, no matter what you do**. You could spend your whole life bending over backward for people, and there will still be someone who's unhappy. That's just life. The sooner you accept this, the sooner you'll be free from the need to constantly seek approval. Your worth isn't tied to how many people like you—it's tied to how much you respect yourself.

6. **Prioritize Your Own Needs**
People-pleasers are great at taking care of others but terrible at taking care of themselves. It's time to flip that script. Start asking yourself, *What do I need?* before saying yes to someone else's request. If helping them is going to leave you drained, stressed, or resentful, it's okay to say no. Your well-being is just as important as theirs.

### WHY BOUNDARIES DON'T MAKE YOU AN A##HOLE

One of the biggest fears people-pleasers have is that setting boundaries will make them seem cold, selfish, or like an a##hole. But here's the reality: **boundaries don't make you selfish—they make you healthy**. When you set boundaries, you're not being rude—you're being clear about what you need to function at your best.

People who respect you will respect your boundaries. The only people who will get mad at you for setting boundaries are the ones who were benefitting from your lack of them. And that's on them, not you.

### YOUR HOMEWORK: THE "NO" CHALLENGE

This week, I want you to take the **"No" Challenge**. Your goal is to say "no" to at least three requests or favors that don't align with your needs, time, or energy. Start small if you need to—maybe it's turning down an invite, declining an extra task at work, or saying no to someone who always leans on you for last-minute help.

When you say "no," pay attention to how it feels. Does it feel empowering? Uncomfortable? Both? The goal here isn't to become a master at saying no overnight—it's to start flexing that muscle and getting comfortable with setting boundaries. After each "no," take a moment to reflect: Did the world end? (Spoiler: it didn't.)

**FINAL THOUGHT**

People-pleasing keeps you trapped in a cycle of resentment, burnout, and self-neglect. It's time to break free from being everyone's doormat and start living for yourself. Learning to say "no" without guilt is one of the most empowering things you can do—and it doesn't make you an a##hole, it makes you someone who respects their own boundaries. You don't owe anyone an explanation for prioritizing your well-being. So, stop living for others' approval, start reclaiming your time and energy, and remember: saying "no" doesn't make you selfish—it makes you f#cking strong.

# 18

# TOXIC RELATIONSHIPS

Toxic relationships—they're like that one splinter you didn't even realize was there until it's buried so deep you can't ignore it anymore. Whether it's a romantic partner, friend, coworker, or even a family member, **toxic people have a way of sucking the life out of you** while making you question whether you're the problem. Spoiler alert: *you're not.*

Toxic relationships are like quicksand—you don't always see the red flags until you're already waist-deep and sinking fast. And by the time you do, you're drained, confused, and wondering how the hell you ended up here. The reality is, **energy vampires** and **sh#tty leeches** have a way of sneaking into your life under the guise of being caring, fun, or supportive, only to slowly reveal their manipulative, draining behavior once you're too invested to easily walk away.

But here's the good news: **you don't have to stay stuck in toxic relationships**. You deserve better—better friends, better partners, better people in your corner. And the first step to clearing out these leeches is spotting the red flags before you're drowning in them. So, let's break down how to spot toxic relationships, cut them out of your life, and finally reclaim your energy, self-worth, and sanity.

**WHAT IS A TOXIC RELATIONSHIP?**

A toxic relationship is any relationship that drains you more than it lifts you. It's characterized by **manipulation, control, criticism, jealousy, and often, gaslighting**. In a toxic relationship, there's usually a power imbalance where one person is constantly taking, and the other is constantly giving—until there's nothing left.

And here's the thing: toxic relationships aren't always obvious. They don't always start with full-blown manipulation or abuse. Often, they begin with subtle control, passive-aggressive comments, or small criticisms that slowly erode your confidence and autonomy over time. You start questioning yourself, bending over backward to please the other person, and making excuses for their behavior. Before you know it, you're stuck in a toxic dynamic, doubting your own reality.

**THE RED FLAGS YOU NEED TO WATCH FOR**

So, how do you spot a toxic relationship before you're drowning in it? Here are the **red flags** to look out for:

1. **They're Always the Victim**
   Toxic people love playing the victim. No matter what happens, it's never their fault—it's always someone else's problem, and they expect you to fix it. They

thrive on guilt trips and make you feel responsible for their emotions, often manipulating you into doing things for them because "you owe them."

2. **Constant Criticism or "Jokes" at Your Expense**
They make "jokes" about your appearance, intelligence, or personality, but when you get upset, they claim you're "too sensitive" or "can't take a joke." Constant criticism—especially under the guise of humor—is a major red flag. Toxic people use this tactic to undermine your self-esteem and keep you feeling small.

3. **Gaslighting**
Gaslighting is one of the most common tactics in toxic relationships. This is when someone manipulates you into questioning your reality. They deny things that happened, twist the truth, or make you feel like you're overreacting or imagining things. The goal is to make you doubt yourself so they can maintain control.

4. **Emotional Manipulation**
They use your emotions against you. Whether it's guilt, fear, or love, toxic people know how to push your buttons to get what they want. They might guilt you into doing things, make you feel bad for setting boundaries, or even use affection as a way to manipulate you into staying in the relationship.

5. **They Suck the Energy Out of You**
Every interaction with them feels draining. After spending time with this person, you feel exhausted, emotionally depleted, and anxious. Instead of uplifting you, they constantly bring drama, negativity, and chaos into your life.

6. **Jealousy and Possessiveness**
In toxic relationships, jealousy is often disguised as love or concern. They might say they're just "looking out for you," but in reality, they're controlling and possessive. They get jealous of your friends, your achievements, or even your happiness and try to isolate you from people who care about you.
7. **They Make Everything About Them**
Every conversation, every problem, and every moment somehow becomes about them. Even when you're going through something difficult, they find a way to make it about their needs, emotions, or struggles. In a toxic relationship, your feelings are often dismissed, ignored, or minimized.

**THE SUBTLE SIGNS YOU'RE ALREADY DROWNING**

Sometimes, toxic relationships don't start with obvious red flags. They creep in, little by little, until you're in too deep to see how much damage it's doing. Here are some subtle signs that you're already drowning in a toxic relationship:

- **You feel like you're walking on eggshells** around them, constantly afraid of saying or doing something that will set them off.
- **You're always apologizing**, even when you haven't done anything wrong.
- **You've become isolated** from friends, family, or activities you once loved because they don't "approve" or make you feel guilty for having a life outside of them.

- **You doubt yourself** constantly—your memory, your decisions, your feelings—because they've made you question your reality.
- **You're emotionally exhausted** all the time and feel like no matter how much you give, it's never enough.

### WHY CUTTING THEM OUT FEELS SO HARD

If you've ever tried to cut a toxic person out of your life, you know it's not easy. In fact, it can feel damn near impossible. Why? Because **toxic people are master manipulators**. They know how to pull you back in just when you're ready to walk away. They'll shower you with affection, make promises to change, or guilt you into staying because they "need" you.

Toxic people feed on your guilt, your fear of conflict, and your empathy. They thrive on keeping you hooked in the relationship because it benefits them. But here's the reality: **you are not responsible for saving, fixing, or carrying someone else's emotional baggage**—especially at the cost of your own well-being. It's hard to walk away, but staying is even harder in the long run.

### HOW TO CUT THE TOXICITY OUT OF YOUR LIFE

If you're ready to cut the toxic people out of your life, here's how to do it:

1. **Set Clear Boundaries**
   Toxic people hate boundaries because it means they can no longer control or manipulate you. But setting

boundaries is the first step to reclaiming your power. Be clear about what you will and won't tolerate—and stick to it. Whether it's limiting contact, saying no to their demands, or refusing to engage in their drama, boundaries are non-negotiable.

2. **Cut the Cord**

In some cases, the only way to truly rid yourself of a toxic person is to cut them off completely. This might mean blocking their number, unfollowing them on social media, or limiting interactions with them to a bare minimum. Yes, it's hard, and yes, they'll try to guilt you back in—but this is about protecting your peace and mental health.

3. **Stop Making Excuses for Their Behavior**

One of the biggest reasons people stay in toxic relationships is because they make excuses for the other person's behavior. Maybe you think, *They've had a hard life* or *They're going through a rough time*. But here's the deal: **their trauma is not your responsibility**. You can have empathy for someone's struggles without letting them treat you like sh#t.

4. **Get Support**

Cutting a toxic person out of your life can feel overwhelming, especially if they've been a big part of it. Surround yourself with people who support you—whether it's friends, family, or even a therapist. You don't have to go through it alone. Having a support system can make it easier to stay strong and resist the urge to go back.

5. **Recognize That You Deserve Better**

The most important step in cutting out toxic relationships is realizing that **you deserve better**. You deserve relationships that lift you up, support you, and make you feel valued—not ones that drain you or tear you down. Once you internalize this truth, it becomes a lot easier to walk away from anyone who doesn't meet that standard.

**YOUR HOMEWORK: THE TOXICITY AUDIT**

This week, I want you to do a **Toxicity Audit**. Take a hard look at the relationships in your life—friends, family, partners, coworkers—and ask yourself: *Are these relationships lifting me up, or are they draining me?* Make a list of anyone who consistently brings negativity, drama, or emotional exhaustion into your life.

Once you have your list, start thinking about how you can set boundaries with those people—or, if necessary, cut them out entirely. The goal isn't to ditch every difficult person in your life overnight, but to start identifying where toxic dynamics exist and take steps to protect yourself. Your energy is valuable—don't waste it on people who don't deserve it.

**FINAL THOUGHT**

Toxic relationships will drain you dry if you let them. The people who manipulate, criticize, and gaslight you aren't just "difficult"—they're damaging. You deserve relationships that nourish and support you, not ones that leave you feeling emotionally bankrupt. So, learn to spot the red flags early, set boundaries like a pro, and cut the leeches and energy vampires out of your life. Because you deserve better—and deep down, you know it.

# 19

# NEED FOR CONTROL

You know that feeling of needing everything to be *just right*? The urge to control every outcome, every detail, and every interaction so nothing slips through the cracks? If you've been living in **control freak mode**, you know how exhausting it is to keep everything locked down 24/7. The constant need to manage every aspect of your life—and sometimes the lives of others—feels like a full-time job, with no time off and no f#cking peace of mind.

But here's the thing: **your need for control is slowly destroying your sanity.** It's making your life sh#t, and it's doing a number on your relationships, happiness, and overall well-being. You think control equals security, but the more you try to micromanage everything, the more you realize that life has a way of reminding you that control is an illusion.

Letting go of control feels like free-falling—it's terrifying. But trying to control everything is like holding sand in your fist—the tighter you grip, the more it slips away. So, in this chapter, we're diving into why you have this obsessive need for control, how it's screwing up your life, and—most importantly—how to loosen the grip and let go without losing your sh#t.

**WHY YOU FEEL THE NEED TO CONTROL EVERYTHING**

Let's get one thing straight: your need for control didn't come out of nowhere. **Control is a response to fear and anxiety**. It's your brain's way of saying, *If I can just control everything, then I'll be safe. Nothing bad will happen. I won't get hurt.* In a world where so much feels unpredictable and out of your hands, control is your way of holding onto some sense of stability.

But here's the catch: **you can't control everything**—no matter how hard you try. Life is full of unknowns, curveballs, and chaos, and no amount of planning or micromanaging will change that. Trying to control everything only fuels more anxiety, because the more you try to lock things down, the more you realize how little you actually control.

The need for control often comes from:

- **Fear of uncertainty**: You want guarantees, and when life doesn't offer them, you try to create your own.
- **Perfectionism**: You feel that things have to be done *your way* or not at all. If it's not perfect, it's not good enough.
- **Fear of failure**: Controlling everything gives you the illusion that you can avoid making mistakes or falling short.

- **Fear of vulnerability**: Letting go means risking emotional exposure, and that's scary as hell.

**THE HIDDEN COST OF BEING A CONTROL FREAK**

On the surface, control might seem like a good thing. After all, being on top of things makes you feel like you're avoiding chaos and failure. But the hidden cost of trying to control everything is enormous. Here's how it's screwing up your life:

1. **You're Exhausted**
   Control is a full-time job, and it's draining as hell. You're constantly planning, overthinking, managing, and redoing everything to make sure it's perfect. No wonder you're always stressed out and running on fumes. You've convinced yourself that if you let go for even a second, things will fall apart—but guess what? *You're falling apart because of it.*
2. **You're Missing Out on Joy**
   When you're always focused on controlling outcomes, you miss the present moment. You're too busy planning the future or fixing problems to enjoy the here and now. Life's spontaneity and unpredictability can be beautiful—if you let it in. But by keeping everything tightly controlled, you're missing the surprises, the fun, and the moments that make life worth living.
3. **You're Straining Your Relationships**
   Nobody likes being micromanaged—whether it's a partner, friend, or coworker. When you're always trying to control situations, people, and outcomes, you push people away. Relationships thrive on trust, not

control. If you're always stepping in to "fix" things or dictate how things should go, you're not leaving room for the people in your life to be themselves.

4. **You're Stuck in a Cycle of Anxiety**

The more you try to control, the more anxious you become. Why? Because you're constantly confronted with the fact that you *can't* control everything. And that realization fuels more anxiety, which makes you try harder to control, and the cycle continues. Instead of giving you peace of mind, control is robbing you of it.

5. **You're Avoiding Growth**

Let's be real: control is about avoiding failure, mistakes, and discomfort. But here's the truth: **growth comes from letting go and allowing yourself to be vulnerable, make mistakes, and learn from them**. When you're obsessed with controlling everything, you're stifling your own growth. You're staying in your comfort zone, where everything feels "safe," but you're not allowing yourself to experience the fullness of life.

**THE ILLUSION OF CONTROL: WHY LETTING GO IS FREEDOM**

The thing about control is that it's an illusion. You think you're keeping everything under wraps, but life has a way of showing you that you can't predict, manage, or prevent every outcome. And honestly, thank f#ck for that. Because when you finally realize that control is an illusion, you can start to let go—and **that's where the real freedom comes in**.

Letting go doesn't mean letting your life fall into chaos. It means recognizing what's in your control (your reactions, your mindset, your decisions) and what's not (other people's actions, the future, circumstances outside your control). Letting go is about **trusting yourself to handle whatever comes** instead of trying to avoid every potential problem.

### HOW TO LET GO OF CONTROL WITHOUT LOSING YOUR SH#T

Ready to loosen the grip and stop letting your need for control run your life? Here's how to do it:

1. **Recognize What You *Can* Control**
   The first step to letting go of control is accepting that there are things you simply can't control. You can't control the weather, other people's choices, or how every situation will play out. But you *can* control your reactions, your mindset, and your actions. Focus on what's in your hands and let go of the rest.
2. **Embrace Uncertainty**
   Uncertainty is scary because it feels like stepping into the unknown. But uncertainty is a part of life—and no amount of control will change that. Start reframing uncertainty as an opportunity rather than a threat. When you let go of needing everything to go a certain way, you open yourself up to new possibilities and experiences that you wouldn't have anticipated.
3. **Practice Letting Go in Small Steps**
   You don't have to go from control freak to free spirit overnight. Start small. Pick one area of your life where you tend to overcontrol—maybe it's your work, your

schedule, or even how you plan your weekends. Consciously allow yourself to loosen the reins. Let someone else make a decision, or allow for flexibility in your plans. Notice how it feels when you step back and things still run smoothly without your interference.

4. **Stop Obsessing Over Perfection**

Perfectionism is a close cousin of control. You think that if everything's perfect, nothing will go wrong. But perfection is unattainable and exhausting. Start embracing the idea that "good enough" is just that—*good enough*. You don't need everything to be perfect to feel safe or successful.

5. **Get Comfortable with Discomfort**

Letting go of control is uncomfortable—there's no way around it. But instead of running from that discomfort, learn to sit with it. When things don't go as planned, or when you're faced with uncertainty, remind yourself that you're capable of handling it. The discomfort of letting go is temporary, but the freedom that comes with it is long-lasting.

6. **Trust Yourself**

At the heart of the need for control is a lack of trust—in the world, in others, and in yourself. You don't trust that things will turn out okay unless you're in charge. But here's the thing: **you're stronger and more capable than you give yourself credit for**. Trust that no matter what happens, you'll figure it out. Letting go isn't about everything going perfectly—it's about knowing that you can handle it even when it doesn't.

**YOUR HOMEWORK: THE "LET GO" CHALLENGE**

This week, I want you to take the **"Let Go" Challenge**. Pick one specific area of your life where you tend to micromanage or over-control. Maybe it's work, your relationship, or even something as simple as your morning routine. Consciously loosen the grip—allow things to unfold without trying to control every detail. Trust that it will work out, even if it's not exactly how you planned.

After you've done it, reflect on how it felt to let go. Did the world fall apart? Or did things actually go more smoothly than you expected? The goal here is to start small, practice letting go, and build trust in yourself and the process.

**FINAL THOUGHT**

Your need for control is driven by fear—the fear that if you let go, everything will fall apart. But the truth is, **the more you try to control, the more chaos you create**. Letting go doesn't mean losing control—it means trusting yourself to handle whatever life throws at you. Stop holding on so tightly, loosen the grip, and allow yourself the freedom to live without the constant weight of trying to control everything. Because when you finally let go, you'll find that life has a way of working itself out—sometimes in ways even better than you could have planned.

# 20

# FEAR OF CONFRONTATION

Let's get one thing straight: **confrontation isn't fun for most people**. If you're like a lot of us, the thought of having a difficult conversation makes your stomach churn and your palms sweat. Whether it's bringing up an issue with a partner, setting boundaries with a friend, or calling someone out for being an a##hole at work, confrontation feels like walking into a battlezone without a weapon.

The fear of confrontation can lead you to avoid difficult conversations altogether. You convince yourself it's not worth the drama, and you'd rather bite your tongue than risk an argument. But here's the thing: **avoiding conflict doesn't make it go away—it just buries it**. And eventually, those unresolved issues will come back to bite you in the a##, whether it's through built-up resentment, passive-aggressive behavior, or explosive arguments that could have been avoided.

But confrontation doesn't have to be a death sentence. It doesn't have to end in a full-blown screaming match or awkward silence. In fact, learning to handle conflict with confidence can actually improve your relationships, reduce stress, and help you feel more in control. This chapter is all about tackling your fear of confrontation head-on and learning how to have the hard conversations without spiraling into a panic attack or losing your sh#t.

**WHY CONFRONTATION FEELS SO DAMN SCARY**

So, why does confrontation feel like you're about to step into a cage match with Mike Tyson? **Fear of confrontation** usually boils down to one of three things:

1. **Fear of Rejection**
   You're terrified that bringing up an issue will make someone dislike you or even abandon you. You're worried that if you rock the boat, the relationship will crumble or they'll hold it against you forever. You'd rather keep the peace than risk rejection.
2. **Fear of Conflict Escalation**
   You don't want a simple disagreement to turn into a full-on war. You're scared that the moment you say something, things will spiral out of control—voices will raise, emotions will flare, and you'll end up in a blowout that leaves both parties angry and disconnected.
3. **Fear of Losing Control**
   Whether it's because you tend to bottle up your emotions until they explode, or because conflict triggers anxiety and panic, you're afraid that once the con-

frontation starts, you'll either go off the rails or completely shut down.

These fears keep you locked in avoidance mode, convinced that conflict is too dangerous to deal with. But here's the truth: **conflict is inevitable**. You can't avoid it forever, and when handled well, confrontation can actually lead to deeper understanding, growth, and stronger relationships. The trick isn't avoiding conflict—it's learning how to approach it without losing your mind (or your temper).

**THE MYTH OF "NICE" VS. "CONFRONTATIONAL"**

Part of why you're terrified of confrontation is that you've been sold this idea that **being "nice" means avoiding conflict**. You think that if you're agreeable, easygoing, and always pleasant, you'll be liked and loved. But avoiding confrontation doesn't make you "nice"—it makes you **repressed**. It builds resentment and frustration until eventually, you either explode in anger or collapse under the weight of your own emotional exhaustion.

Being **assertive** doesn't make you a jerk, and being **honest** doesn't make you aggressive. In fact, people who can handle conflict maturely are often more respected because they know how to speak up for themselves without causing chaos. You don't have to choose between being "nice" and standing up for yourself—you can do both. You just need the tools.

## WHY AVOIDING CONFRONTATION IS F#CKING YOU OVER

You might think avoiding confrontation is the "peaceful" option, but here's why it's actually screwing you over:

1. **Resentment Builds**
   Every time you avoid speaking up, you're burying your feelings. And the more you bury them, the more resentment builds. What starts as a minor irritation turns into full-blown bitterness, and eventually, you start resenting the people around you for things they didn't even realize were an issue.
2. **Problems Get Worse**
   Avoiding conflict doesn't solve problems—it gives them room to grow. Ignored issues fester, and what could have been a simple conversation turns into a bigger issue because it wasn't addressed early on. The longer you avoid confrontation, the bigger the mess becomes.
3. **You Lose Your Sense of Self**
   When you consistently avoid confrontation, you stop advocating for your needs, values, and boundaries. Over time, you start losing touch with who you are because you've been too busy tiptoeing around everyone else's feelings. You end up feeling powerless and frustrated, and that leads to burnout.

## HOW TO HAVE THE HARD CONVERSATIONS WITHOUT SPIRALING

Ready to tackle your fear of confrontation and stop letting conflict control your life? Here's how to have difficult conversations without spiraling into a panic attack or blackout rage:

1. **Prepare Mentally**
   Before you jump into a confrontation, take a minute to mentally prepare. Ask yourself: *What's my goal?* Are you looking to resolve a specific issue, set a boundary, or express how you feel? Focus on the outcome you want instead of obsessing over the potential drama. Preparation gives you clarity and helps you stay calm when emotions run high.
2. **Choose the Right Time**
   Timing is everything. Don't start a confrontation when you're furious, tired, or in the middle of a public place. Pick a time and setting where you can have the conversation calmly and privately. The last thing you want is to confront someone when you're already on edge or when they're distracted and defensive.
3. **Use "I" Statements**
   When you finally start the conversation, frame things from your perspective using "I" statements. Instead of saying, *"You always ignore me,"* try saying, *"I feel hurt when I don't get a response from you."* This approach makes it less accusatory and more about how you're feeling. It reduces defensiveness and makes it easier for the other person to hear you.
4. **Stay Calm (Even When You Want to Scream)**
   One of the hardest parts of confrontation is keeping your cool. When you're upset, it's easy to let your emotions take over, but staying calm is crucial. If you feel yourself getting worked up, take a deep breath, and remind yourself that you're here to resolve the issue—not escalate it. If things start to heat up, don't

be afraid to take a pause and regroup before continuing the conversation.

5. **Be Direct, Not Aggressive**
There's a difference between being assertive and being aggressive. Assertiveness is about clearly stating your needs and boundaries in a respectful way, while aggression is about overpowering or attacking the other person. Stick to the facts, focus on how you feel, and avoid personal attacks. You can be direct without being a d#ck.

6. **Listen as Much as You Speak**
Confrontation isn't just about you getting your point across—it's also about listening to the other person's perspective. You may be surprised to find that there's a misunderstanding or a different side to the story you hadn't considered. Give them space to speak, and listen without interrupting. Real resolution comes from mutual understanding.

7. **Know When to Walk Away**
Not every confrontation is going to end in a resolution, and that's okay. Sometimes, the other person isn't willing to hear you out or compromise. If the conversation starts to go off the rails, or if you're being disrespected, it's okay to walk away. You're not obligated to stick around and endure a toxic argument. Walking away doesn't mean you've failed—it means you're protecting your peace.

### WHY CONFLICT CAN ACTUALLY BE GOOD FOR YOU

Here's the wild truth: **conflict isn't always a bad thing**. In fact, when handled well, conflict can strengthen relationships and lead to deeper understanding. Healthy confrontation can clear the air, set boundaries, and create space for both parties to grow. It's not about "winning" or proving who's right—it's about finding common ground and resolving issues before they turn into bigger problems.

The next time you're tempted to avoid a confrontation, remind yourself that conflict can be a tool for growth. It's a way to address issues head-on and make your relationships stronger—not something to fear or run from.

**YOUR HOMEWORK: THE "SPEAK UP" CHALLENGE**

This week, instead of diving headfirst into a full-on confrontation, try the **"Speak Up" Challenge**. Pick a low-stakes situation where you'd normally stay quiet to avoid conflict—maybe someone cutting in line, a coworker dismissing your idea, or a friend making a joke at your expense. Instead of letting it slide, **speak up**. It doesn't have to be a major confrontation—just a simple, direct statement that expresses how you feel.

For example, say something like, *"Actually, I was next in line,"* or *"That comment bothered me."* Focus on being calm and assertive without turning it into an argument. Afterward,

**FINAL THOUGHT**

Fear of confrontation keeps you stuck in a cycle of avoidance, resentment, and unspoken issues. But confrontation isn't a death sentence—it's a tool for clearing the air, setting boundaries, and standing up for yourself. By learning to approach conflict with confidence, you'll not only stop spiraling into panic, but you'll also strengthen your relationships and reclaim your voice. So, stop running from confrontation, embrace the uncomfortable, and remember: conflict doesn't have to be a battle—it can be a step toward growth.

# PART 3: OWNING YOUR SH#T

# 21

# SELF-WORTH

How many times have you caught yourself waiting for someone else to validate you? You're waiting for the universe—or a boss, a friend, a partner, *anyone*—to give you the green light to feel good about yourself. **News flash: you don't need anyone's f#cking permission** to be awesome. You never did. But somehow, along the way, you convinced yourself that your worth is something to be earned, proven, or bestowed upon you by others. Spoiler: *it's not.* You've been worthy all along, but believing it? That's where the work comes in.

**Self-worth** is a tricky beast. It's not about what you accomplish, how you look, or what others think of you. It's about recognizing that you are enough as you are—flaws, failures, and all. It's about stepping into your f#cking greatness without waiting for external validation. This chapter is about smashing the idea that you need permission to feel worthy and learning how to truly believe in your inherent awesomeness—because it's time to stop sleeping on yourself.

## WHY YOU KEEP WAITING FOR PERMISSION

So why do we wait for permission to feel worthy? It usually comes down to one or more of the following:

1. **You've Been Conditioned to Seek Approval**
   From a young age, we're taught to look outside ourselves for validation. Good grades, compliments from others, praise from authority figures—our self-worth becomes tied to external approval. You start believing that if people aren't constantly affirming your worth, maybe it doesn't exist.

2. **You Compare Yourself to Others**
   Social media is a breeding ground for self-doubt. You scroll through feeds, seeing people who seem more successful, better looking, more accomplished, and living the life you think you *should* be living. So, instead of recognizing your own worth, you convince yourself that you're falling short.

3. **You Think Your Worth Is Based on Achievement**
   Society loves to tie self-worth to productivity. You're taught that your value lies in what you achieve—whether it's your job, your accolades, or how busy you are. If you're not constantly "proving" yourself through accomplishments, you start feeling like you're not enough.

4. **You're Waiting for Someone to Validate You**
   Maybe you've convinced yourself that you'll finally feel worthy when someone tells you you're enough—whether it's a partner who loves you, a boss who promotes you, or a friend who praises you. But relying on external validation is a never-ending trap.

If you're always waiting for someone else to tell you you're worthy, you'll never feel it on your own.

### THE BULLSH#T MYTH OF "EARNED" WORTH

Here's the thing: **self-worth isn't something you have to earn**. It's not a prize you get when you've accomplished enough, looked a certain way, or made everyone happy. Self-worth is inherent. It's f#cking built-in. You were born worthy—end of story. But somewhere along the way, society convinced you that you need to hustle for your worthiness, to constantly prove that you deserve love, success, or happiness.

This myth of "earned" worth keeps you in a cycle of constant striving, always thinking, *I'll be worthy when...* When you land the perfect job, when you lose the weight, when you get into a relationship, when you achieve something "big." But here's the truth: **you don't need to "become" worthy—you already are**. Your worth is not conditional. It's not something you need to prove. It's time to start owning it.

### WHY SELF-WORTH MATTERS

When you believe in your own worth, everything changes. **Self-worth is the foundation of your confidence, your boundaries, and your happiness**. It's the difference between chasing validation and standing firm in your own awesomeness. It's the fuel that powers your ability to say no, to walk away from sh#tty situations, and to demand the respect you deserve.

Without self-worth, you're constantly at the mercy of others' opinions. You let people walk all over you because you don't believe you're worthy of standing up for yourself. You stay in toxic relationships, dead-end jobs, or situations that drain you because you don't believe you deserve better. But when you start believing in your inherent worth, you stop settling. You start making decisions that align with your value, not someone else's approval.

### HOW TO START BELIEVING IN YOUR WORTH—RIGHT NOW

Ready to stop waiting for permission and start owning your worth? Here's how to do it:

1.  **Recognize That Your Worth Is Inherent**
    First things first: **your worth is not tied to anything external**—not your job, your looks, your achievements, or your relationships. Your worth is innate. It's not something you earn; it's something you already have. Start telling yourself that every day. Write it down. Say it out loud. Tattoo it on your f#cking soul: *I am worthy as I am.*
2.  **Stop Comparing Yourself to Others**
    The comparison trap is a thief of self-worth. The more you compare yourself to others, the more you start questioning your own value. But here's the thing: **someone else's success or beauty doesn't diminish yours**. There's enough greatness to go around, and your journey is yours alone. Stop measuring your worth by someone else's path.
3.  **Set Boundaries Like a Boss**
    People with low self-worth let others walk all over

them. Why? Because they don't believe they deserve better. But guess what? **You deserve f#cking respect**. Start setting boundaries in your life—whether it's at work, in relationships, or with friends. Boundaries are a reflection of self-worth. When you set them, you're saying, *I matter. My needs matter.* And you do.

4. **Celebrate Your Wins—Even the Small Ones**
One of the reasons you don't feel worthy is because you're so focused on what you *haven't* accomplished that you forget to acknowledge what you *have*. Start celebrating your wins—big and small. Maybe you crushed it at work today. Maybe you worked out when you didn't feel like it. Maybe you took time for yourself when you needed it. Every time you acknowledge your achievements, you reinforce the belief that you're capable and worthy.

5. **Let Go of Needing Approval**
You don't need anyone else's approval to be f#cking awesome. Stop waiting for someone to tell you that you're enough. You already are. And the people who matter? They'll see it too. The people who don't? They can f#ck off. When you let go of needing external validation, you start living for yourself—not for what others think of you.

6. **Practice Self-Compassion**
Start treating yourself like you would a friend. You wouldn't tell your friend they're worthless because they didn't land a job or because they gained a few pounds, right? So why the hell are you doing it to yourself? **Self-compassion** is key to building self-worth. Be kind to yourself, especially when you f#ck

up. You're not perfect, but that doesn't mean you're not worthy.

## PERMISSION SLIPS ARE FOR SCHOOL—NOT YOUR SELF-WORTH

You don't need permission to feel worthy. You don't need to ask anyone for approval to be f#cking awesome. **You already are**. The only thing standing between you and owning that fact is your mindset. You've been conditioned to believe that your worth is something you have to earn, but that's bullsh#t. It's time to stop waiting for someone else to give you the green light to love yourself and start recognizing that you've been enough all along.

### YOUR HOMEWORK: THE "I AM WORTHY" RITUAL

This week, I want you to create an **"I Am Worthy" Ritual**. Every day, I want you to look in the mirror and say out loud: *"I am f#cking worthy."* I don't care if it feels awkward, cheesy, or ridiculous—do it anyway. Write it down if that helps. Put it on a sticky note on your fridge, or set a reminder on your phone. The goal is to **retrain your brain to believe in your worth**. You don't need a reason to feel worthy—you already are.

At the end of the week, reflect on how this exercise felt. Did it shift your mindset? Did you feel more empowered? The goal here isn't to magically "fix" your self-worth overnight, but to start reinforcing the truth: you are enough, as you are, without needing anyone else's permission.

**FINAL THOUGHT**

Self-worth isn't something you have to hustle for or prove—it's already yours. You don't need permission to be f#cking awesome because you already are. It's time to stop waiting for external validation and start believing in your inherent worth. When you own your self-worth, you stop living for others' approval and start living for yourself. And when you do that? **You're unstoppable**.

# 22

# FOMO (FEAR OF MISSING OUT)

Let's be honest—**FOMO** (Fear of Missing Out) is that little voice in your head that won't shut the hell up. It's what makes you feel like you're always one step behind, that everyone else is out there living their best lives while you're stuck at home in your sweatpants. You scroll through Instagram, see people at concerts, parties, tropical vacations, or trendy brunch spots, and suddenly you're convinced that your life is a dumpster fire. **Sound familiar?**

Here's the truth you need to hear: **you're not missing sh#t**. FOMO is just your brain's way of screwing with you, convincing you that everyone else is out there having life-changing experiences while you're "missing out." But chasing every experience doesn't lead to happiness—it leads to burnout, stress, and a constant sense of not being enough. This chapter is about breaking free from the toxic cycle of FOMO and realizing that you don't need to be everywhere, doing everything, to live a happy, fulfilled life.

### WHAT FOMO REALLY IS (AND WHY IT'S BULLSH#T)

FOMO isn't about actually missing out on anything important—it's about **fear**. Fear that you're not doing enough. Fear that you're not living up to some imaginary standard of what life *should* look like. Fear that everyone else has their sh#t together and you're falling behind.

FOMO is fueled by two things: **comparison** and **perfectionism**. You compare your everyday life to someone else's highlight reel and suddenly feel like you're not measuring up. But here's the kicker: **most of what you see online is a f#cking illusion**. Those perfect photos? They're carefully curated, edited, and filtered to show only the best moments, while all the messy, boring, or uncomfortable parts are left out. You're comparing your full, unfiltered life to someone else's staged, filtered snapshot. It's a losing game.

FOMO convinces you that you're missing out on happiness, but the truth is, **chasing every experience won't make you happy**—it'll just make you anxious and unsatisfied.

### THE SOCIAL MEDIA TRAP

Let's call it what it is: **social media is FOMO's breeding ground**. It's where you go to be reminded, constantly, that you're "not doing enough." Every scroll brings another reminder that you're not at that event, that you didn't book that vacation, that you're not hanging out with that group. But here's the thing: social media is a curated highlight reel, not real life.

People post their best moments, their peak experiences. They don't post the boring, awkward, or downright shitty parts. No one's showing you their Monday morning blues, their relationship fights, or the fact that they spent last weekend binging Netflix and eating takeout. Yet somehow, you convince yourself that everyone else is out there living an epic life 24/7, while you're stuck in mediocrity.

Here's the truth: **no one is living an exciting life all the time.** Not even the influencers you idolize. Everyone has downtime, struggles, and quiet moments. And honestly? You don't need to document every moment of your life online either.

**WHY CHASING EVERY EXPERIENCE WILL BURN YOU OUT**

FOMO tells you that you should say "yes" to everything—that every missed opportunity is a loss. But what it doesn't tell you is that **chasing every experience is f#cking exhausting**. Trying to be everywhere, doing everything, all the time leads to burnout. You're constantly on the move, filling your schedule with plans, and pushing yourself to "keep up" with the crowd, only to find that the more you do, the less fulfilled you feel.

**The more you chase, the more empty you feel.** That's because happiness doesn't come from having a packed social calendar or hitting every event—it comes from being intentional with your time, focusing on the experiences and people that actually bring you joy and meaning. When you're always in FOMO mode, you're never fully present in the moment because you're already thinking about the next thing, the next event, the next opportunity you can't miss. **That's not living—that's running.**

### WHY YOU'RE NOT MISSING ANYTHING IMPORTANT

Here's the truth: **you're not missing out on anything that truly matters.** The experiences that are right for you, the people who are meant to be in your life, and the opportunities that align with your values will always find their way to you. You don't need to chase them. The things that are meant for you won't pass you by.

FOMO convinces you that every missed event is a missed opportunity for happiness. But happiness isn't found in cramming your schedule full of social events or trying to keep up with everyone else's plans. Happiness comes from **being fully present in your own life**, not from chasing someone else's version of it.

You don't need to be at every party, attend every networking event, or say yes to every invite just to feel like you're living a fulfilling life. The life that's meaningful to *you* is the one that brings you peace, joy, and satisfaction—even if it looks quieter or less glamorous than what's plastered all over social media.

### HOW TO BREAK FREE FROM FOMO

Ready to stop letting FOMO run your life? Here's how to break free from the toxic cycle of always feeling like you're missing out:

1.  **Unplug from Social Media**
    FOMO thrives on social media, so take a break. Set boundaries for how much time you spend scrolling, or go on a full social media detox for a few days. Trust me, the world will keep turning, and you'll feel a whole lot better without the constant comparison to everyone else's highlight reels.
2.  **Focus on What *You* Want**
    Stop asking yourself what you "should" be doing and start asking yourself what you actually *want* to be doing. Do you really want to go to that event, or are you just going because you don't want to feel left out? Get clear on what activities, experiences, and people bring you joy, and focus on those. The rest? Let it go.
3.  **Practice Saying "No"**
    FOMO makes you feel like saying "no" is a failure, but in reality, saying "no" is one of the most empowering things you can do. You don't have to attend every event, meet up with everyone, or say yes to every opportunity. Start practicing saying "no" to the things that don't align with your priorities. You'll feel less stressed, more in control, and way more fulfilled.
4.  **Be Present in Your Own Life**
    FOMO pulls you out of the present moment, making you think about what you're missing instead of enjoying where you are. Practice being present—whether you're at home, out with friends, or even just relaxing solo. **Your life is happening right now**—don't miss it because you're too busy worrying about what everyone else is doing.
5.  **Trust That What's Meant for You Won't Pass You By**
    The fear that you're missing out is rooted in the belief

that if you don't do everything, you'll miss something important. But here's the truth: **what's meant for you will find you**. You don't have to chase every experience or constantly keep up with everyone else. The right opportunities, connections, and experiences will come to you when the time is right.

**YOUR HOMEWORK: THE "F#CK FOMO" EXPERIMENT**

This week, I want you to do a little experiment: the **"F#ck FOMO" Experiment**. Every time you catch yourself feeling FOMO—whether it's from seeing something on social media or hearing about an event—pause. Ask yourself, *Am I actually missing out on something that will bring me joy or fulfillment, or am I just reacting to the fear of missing out?*

For one week, commit to **saying "no" to things that don't truly align with your values or desires**. Instead of chasing every experience, focus on the ones that matter to you. At the end of the week, reflect: Did you actually miss out on anything important? Or did you find that you were more present, less stressed, and more content with the life you're living?

**FINAL THOUGHT**

FOMO is a f#cking lie. It convinces you that you need to chase every experience, say yes to every opportunity, and always be on the go to live a meaningful life. But the truth is, **you're not missing sh#t**. You don't need to be everywhere, doing everything, to be happy. The life that matters is the one you're living right now, in the present, not the one you're constantly chasing. So, stop letting FOMO run the show, start being intentional with your time, and remember: **you're exactly where you're meant to be**.

# 23

# FEAR OF CHANGE

Change. The very word probably makes your stomach clench a little. It's the thing we all know is inevitable, yet most of us try to avoid like the plague. Whether it's a major life shift—like moving to a new city, starting a new job, or ending a relationship—or just the everyday changes that come with growing up, **change is f#cking terrifying**. But here's the hard truth: **staying stuck in the same place forever isn't an option**. Change will happen, whether you like it or not, and clinging to the past out of fear is a sure way to keep yourself from growing.

This chapter is all about tackling the fear of change head-on and embracing the fact that life is in a constant state of flux. You can't avoid it, you can't stop it, and honestly, you shouldn't even want to. **Change is how you grow, evolve, and become the person you're meant to be**—even if the process scares the sh#t out of you.

### WHY CHANGE SCARES THE HELL OUT OF YOU

So why does change feel like stepping off a cliff into the unknown? It's because **change is deeply uncomfort-**

**able**. We're wired to seek comfort, predictability, and stability. Staying in familiar territory, even if it sucks, feels safer than stepping into the unknown, where anything could happen.

Here's why change freaks you out:

1. **Fear of the Unknown**
   Change means stepping into uncertainty, and uncertainty is uncomfortable. You don't know what's going to happen, and that lack of control makes your brain go into panic mode. What if it all goes wrong? What if you fail? The unknown triggers your fear response, even if the change could be for the better.
2. **Comfort Zones Are Addictive**
   Let's face it—**comfort zones are like a cozy prison**. They're familiar, predictable, and they don't challenge you. But they're also limiting as hell. When you've been stuck in the same routine, job, relationship, or mindset for a long time, stepping out of it feels like leaving your security blanket behind. Even if your comfort zone isn't serving you, the fear of stepping out into the unknown keeps you clinging to it.
3. **You're Afraid of Failure**
   Change often comes with risk. Whether it's starting something new or letting go of something old, there's always the possibility of failure. And failure? That sh#t is scary. You worry that if you make a change and it doesn't work out, you'll be worse off than you were before. So, you stay stuck, telling yourself that at least the devil you know is better than the devil you don't.

4. **You're Attached to Your Old Identity**
Change often requires shedding parts of your old self. Maybe it's leaving behind an identity tied to a job, a relationship, or a certain phase of life. And that's tough. You've spent years building this version of yourself, and letting go of it can feel like losing a part of who you are. But here's the truth: **you're not meant to stay the same forever.** Your old identity served you at one point, but you're allowed to grow and evolve.

**THE MYTH OF STAYING IN ONE PLACE**

We like to believe that if we just hold on tightly enough, we can keep things the way they are. But **staying the same is an illusion.** Whether you realize it or not, change is happening all the time. Even when you think you're stuck, you're still changing—just not in ways that serve you. You might be growing more complacent, more frustrated, more disconnected from the life you actually want to live.

The reality is, **staying in one place is never an option.** Life moves forward whether you're ready or not. The choice isn't between change or no change—it's between growth or stagnation. And staying stuck in the same place out of fear is just a slower, more painful kind of change that drags you down.

**WHY YOU CAN'T STAY STUCK FOREVER**

You might think you're protecting yourself by avoiding change, but here's the truth: **staying stuck is far more**

**dangerous** than taking a risk and embracing change. When you resist change, you're not protecting yourself—you're limiting yourself. You're holding back from opportunities that could bring you happiness, growth, and fulfillment.

Here's why staying stuck is a losing game:

1. **Life Moves On Without You**
   The world keeps turning, people keep growing, and opportunities keep coming—even if you're not ready to move with them. Staying in one place doesn't stop time, it just leaves you behind. You risk waking up one day and realizing that life has passed you by while you were too busy clinging to the past.
2. **Stagnation Breeds Resentment**
   When you stay stuck for too long, you start to feel it in your bones. You get restless, frustrated, and resentful—at yourself, at others, and at life in general. You know you're capable of more, but fear is keeping you from going after it. That resentment only builds over time, leaving you feeling trapped and bitter.
3. **Growth Only Happens Outside Your Comfort Zone**
   Real growth doesn't happen when everything is smooth and easy. It happens when you challenge yourself, take risks, and embrace discomfort. **Your comfort zone might feel safe, but it's also where your potential goes to die.** Every time you push yourself outside of it, you grow stronger, smarter, and more capable of handling whatever comes next.

4. **Change Is the Key to Becoming Who You're Meant to Be**
The person you're meant to become isn't the person you are right now. **Change is the bridge that takes you from where you are to where you want to be.** Whether it's a career change, a relationship shift, or a mindset overhaul, embracing change is how you evolve into the best version of yourself. Staying stuck only delays the inevitable.

**HOW TO EMBRACE CHANGE WITHOUT LOSING YOUR SH#T**

So, how do you start embracing change instead of running from it? Here's how to move forward—even when it's terrifying:

1. **Acknowledge the Fear**
First things first: **it's okay to be scared of change.** Fear is a normal response to uncertainty, and there's no point in pretending it doesn't exist. The key is not letting that fear control you. Acknowledge it, feel it, and then make the decision to move forward anyway. **Courage isn't the absence of fear—it's taking action despite it.**
2. **Start Small**
Change doesn't have to be a giant leap into the unknown. Start with small, manageable changes that push you out of your comfort zone little by little. Maybe it's changing your routine, trying a new hobby, or saying yes to an opportunity you'd usually turn down. The more you practice embracing small changes, the easier it becomes to face the bigger ones.

3. **Focus on What You Can Control**
Change can feel overwhelming because so much of it is out of your control. But here's the good news: **you don't have to control everything—just your response to it**. Focus on what's within your power: your mindset, your actions, and your attitude. When you shift your focus from what you can't control to what you can, change feels less like free-falling and more like navigating.

4. **Let Go of the Need for Certainty**
You're never going to have all the answers before making a change, and that's okay. **Let go of the need for certainty** and start trusting yourself to handle whatever comes next. The unknown is where possibility lives, and the only way to tap into it is to let go of the need for guarantees.

5. **Remember Your "Why"**
Whenever you're faced with a change that scares you, remind yourself why you're making the change in the first place. What's the bigger picture? What's the ultimate goal? **Focusing on your "why" gives you the motivation to push through the fear** and keep moving forward, even when it feels uncomfortable.

6. **Be Patient with Yourself**
Change isn't easy, and it's not supposed to be. It's okay to struggle with it, to feel scared, or even to stumble along the way. **Be patient with yourself** as you navigate the process. Growth doesn't happen overnight, and you don't need to have everything figured out right away.

**YOUR HOMEWORK: THE "EMBRACE CHANGE" CHALLENGE**

This week, I want you to take on the **"Embrace Change" Challenge**. Pick one area of your life where you've been stuck or resisting change—whether it's a job you're unhappy with, a relationship that's run its course, or a personal goal you've been putting off. **Make one small change** in that area, whether it's taking action toward a new goal, letting go of something that no longer serves you, or simply shifting your mindset.

The goal isn't to overhaul your life in one go—it's to practice embracing the discomfort of change. At the end of the week, reflect on how it felt to take that step. Did the world end? (Spoiler: it didn't.) Did you feel more empowered, even in the midst of uncertainty? The more you embrace change, the more you'll realize that it's not as scary as your fear made it out to be.

**FINAL THOUGHT**

Change is inevitable, and resisting it only keeps you stuck in the same place, frustrated and unfulfilled. **You can't stay stuck forever**, no matter how much you want to hold on to the familiar. The good news is, change is also the key to growth, happiness, and becoming the person you're meant to be. So, stop running from it, start embracing it, and remember: **the only constant in life is change—and that's not a bad thing**.

# 24

# GUILT AND SHAME

We've all been there. That moment when you look back at something you did—or didn't do—and cringe so hard you want to crawl into a hole. Whether it's a stupid decision, an embarrassing slip-up, or a massive screw-up that still haunts you, **guilt and shame** are like unwanted houseguests that refuse to leave. They linger in your mind, replaying the worst moments of your life on a loop, constantly reminding you that you f#cked up.

But here's the thing: **your past mistakes don't define you unless you let them**. Guilt and shame are emotional weights that keep you tethered to a version of yourself that no longer exists. And if you don't learn how to let go of your past f#ck-ups, you'll keep carrying them with you, dragging them into your present and future happiness. This chapter is all about how to stop letting guilt and shame control your life, so you can finally release the baggage and move the hell on.

## GUILT VS. SHAME: THE TOXIC DUO

Let's break down the toxic duo that is **guilt** and **shame**. While they're often used interchangeably, they're actually two distinct emotions that do different types of damage:

1. **Guilt** is the feeling that you've done something wrong. It's triggered by specific actions or decisions, and it can be useful—sometimes. Guilt can motivate you to make amends, apologize, or change your behavior. But when it lingers long after the mistake has been made, guilt turns into a burden that weighs you down, constantly whispering, *You should have done better.*
2. **Shame**, on the other hand, is the belief that there's something inherently wrong with *you*. While guilt says, *I did something bad,* shame says, *I am bad.* It's that deep-rooted feeling that you're unworthy, broken, or unlovable because of your mistakes. Shame goes beyond the action and attacks your sense of self-worth, making you feel like your mistakes define who you are.

Both of these emotions, when left unchecked, are toxic as hell. They keep you stuck in the past, make you afraid to move forward, and convince you that you don't deserve happiness, success, or love. But here's the truth: **you are not your past f#ck-ups**. Guilt and shame don't have to be your permanent roommates.

## WHY YOU CAN'T LET GO OF PAST MISTAKES

If guilt and shame are so destructive, why do we cling to them so tightly? It's because we've been conditioned to believe that holding onto them somehow makes us "better" people. You think that if you forgive yourself or let go of the past, it means you're excusing your behavior or pretending it didn't happen. **That's bullsh#t.**

Here are the real reasons you're holding on to guilt and shame:

1. **You Think You Deserve Punishment**
   Deep down, you believe that because you f#cked up, you deserve to feel bad about it—maybe even forever. You're stuck in a cycle of self-punishment, convinced that carrying guilt and shame is your penance. But this is just emotional self-sabotage. Punishing yourself won't fix the past, and it sure as hell won't make you happier.
2. **You Fear Facing the Consequences**
   Sometimes guilt and shame linger because you haven't fully faced the consequences of your actions. Maybe you haven't apologized, made amends, or taken responsibility. The fear of confronting what you did head-on keeps you stuck in a loop of guilt. But here's the thing: *facing your mistakes is the only way to move past them.*
3. **You've Tied Your Identity to Your Mistakes**
   When shame kicks in, it makes you believe that your past mistakes define who you are. You start to think, *I'm the person who always f#cks up. I'm the person who can't get it right.* But this is a lie. Your mistakes

are something you did, not something you are. **You are not your past.**
4. **You Haven't Learned to Forgive Yourself**
Let's be real: forgiving yourself is hard. It's way easier to hold on to the guilt and beat yourself up over what you should've done differently. But forgiveness is the key to freedom. When you refuse to forgive yourself, you're essentially chaining yourself to the past and giving your mistakes power over your present and future.

**THE COST OF CARRYING GUILT AND SHAME**

Holding onto guilt and shame doesn't just keep you stuck in the past—it also f#cks with your present and future happiness. Here's what it costs you to keep dragging that emotional baggage around:

1. **You Sabotage Your Own Happiness**
Guilt and shame tell you that you don't deserve to be happy, so you subconsciously (or even consciously) sabotage yourself. Whether it's pushing away love, holding back from opportunities, or making choices that keep you stuck, you're convinced that you're not worthy of good things because of your past. News flash: *you are.*
2. **You Keep Repeating the Same Mistakes**
When you're stuck in guilt and shame, you're more likely to repeat the same mistakes over and over again. Why? Because you haven't learned to let go and grow. You're still defining yourself by your past behavior, which means you're stuck in the same pat-

terns. Breaking the cycle means learning from your mistakes—not wallowing in them.
3. **You Miss Out on Growth and Healing**
Guilt and shame block you from moving forward. When you're consumed by these emotions, you're too busy beating yourself up to focus on growth, healing, or self-improvement. Letting go isn't about forgetting what happened—it's about learning the lesson and then moving the f#ck on.
4. **You Block Yourself from Meaningful Relationships**
Carrying guilt and shame into your relationships creates walls between you and the people who care about you. Whether it's because you're afraid of being vulnerable or because you think you don't deserve love, guilt and shame isolate you. But **you deserve love and connection**, no matter what your past looks like.

### HOW TO LET GO OF GUILT AND SHAME

Ready to let go of the past and stop letting guilt and shame f#ck with your future? Here's how to start shedding that emotional baggage:

1. **Acknowledge What Happened**
The first step to letting go is facing your mistakes head-on. Acknowledge what you did (or didn't do) and take responsibility for it. Ignoring it or pretending it didn't happen only prolongs the guilt. Be real with yourself about what went down, but don't confuse acknowledgment with punishment.

2. **Make Amends Where You Can**

    If your mistake hurt someone else, making amends is crucial. Whether it's apologizing, making things right, or taking accountability, **facing the consequences** of your actions is the key to moving forward. You can't change the past, but you can take responsibility for it. And once you've made amends, you've done your part—it's time to let it go.

3. **Forgive Yourself**

    Here's the hard part: **forgiving yourself**. This doesn't mean excusing your behavior or pretending it didn't matter—it means recognizing that you're human, you made a mistake, and you're allowed to move on. Forgiveness is about releasing the emotional hold that guilt and shame have over you. It's about giving yourself permission to be imperfect.

4. **Learn the Lesson**

    Every mistake comes with a lesson, and part of letting go is learning what that lesson is. Ask yourself: *What can I take away from this experience? How can I grow from it?* Once you've learned the lesson, the mistake has served its purpose. There's no reason to keep punishing yourself for something that has already taught you what you needed to know.

5. **Stop Defining Yourself by Your Past**

    The biggest lie guilt and shame tell you is that your past defines you. It doesn't. **You are not your mistakes.** You are a complex, evolving human being who is capable of growth, change, and redemption. Start defining yourself by who you are today and who you're becoming—not by who you were when you f#cked up.

## YOUR HOMEWORK: THE "FORGIVE AND RELEASE" RITUAL

This week, I want you to try the **"Forgive and Release" Ritual**. Find a quiet space where you won't be interrupted, and write down one major mistake or moment of guilt and shame that you've been carrying. Write out how it's made you feel, what you've learned from it, and how it's been holding you back.

Once you've written it all down, **say out loud**: *I forgive myself for this, and I release it.* Then either tear the paper into pieces or burn it (safely, of course). The goal here is to **symbolically let go** of the emotional weight you've been carrying. It may sound simple, but the act of writing, forgiving, and physically releasing the past can be incredibly powerful.

### FINAL THOUGHT

Guilt and shame are emotional anchors that keep you tied to a version of yourself that no longer exists. **You did f#ck up—so what?** We all do. Your mistakes don't define you, but holding onto guilt and shame will if you let it. It's time to forgive yourself, learn the lesson, and move the hell on. **Your future deserves a lighter, freer version of you**—one that isn't weighed down by the ghosts of your past. Stop letting guilt and shame control your happiness, because, trust me, **you've earned the right to let go.**

# 25

# PERCEIVED WEAKNESS

Let's talk about **weakness**. Society has a way of convincing you that certain traits or vulnerabilities make you weak, flawed, or less capable. Whether it's your sensitivity, your introversion, your anxiety, or any other trait you've been conditioned to see as a liability, you've probably spent a good chunk of your life trying to hide or "fix" these parts of yourself. But here's the reality: **the things you think make you weak might actually be your greatest f#cking superpowers**.

**Perceived weakness** is just that—*perceived*. It's a story you've been telling yourself, or a message you've absorbed from a world that values strength in a narrow, shallow way. The truth is, the traits that you've labeled as weaknesses are often what make you *uniquely* strong. Vulnerabilities aren't flaws to be erased; they're powerful aspects of who you are that, when embraced, can become your biggest assets.

This chapter is about flipping the script on weakness, embracing your vulnerabilities, and realizing that the traits you've been hiding are the very things that make you f#cking powerful.

### THE BULLSH#T MYTH OF "WEAKNESS"

The reason we're so quick to label certain traits as weaknesses is because we live in a society that worships **a narrow definition of strength**. You're taught that to be strong means being confident, outgoing, fearless, and always in control. But what about the quieter forms of strength? What about the resilience in vulnerability, the courage in self-reflection, the power in empathy?

Society loves to celebrate external, performative strength, but **real strength** comes in many forms—some of which look a lot like what people call "weakness." Sensitivity, for example, is often seen as fragile or soft, but the ability to deeply feel and understand emotions is a superpower. **Anxiety** might seem like a burden, but it also makes you hyper-aware, cautious, and prepared. **Introversion** isn't a flaw; it's a wellspring of creativity and thoughtfulness.

The point is, **"weakness" is a myth**. The traits you've been taught to suppress or apologize for aren't weaknesses at all—they're the foundation of your greatest strengths. And it's time to stop seeing them as liabilities and start recognizing them as the superpowers they are.

## THE VULNERABILITY PARADOX: WHY WEAKNESS IS STRENGTH

Here's the paradox: **what you perceive as weakness is often the source of your greatest strength**. Vulnerability—the very thing you're terrified of exposing—is a pathway to deeper connection, growth, and authentic power. When you allow yourself to be vulnerable, you open the door to growth in a way that pretending to be "strong" never will.

Brené Brown, vulnerability researcher and all-around badass, says it best: **"Vulnerability is not winning or losing; it's having the courage to show up and be seen when we have no control over the outcome."** That's strength. The ability to show up in the face of fear, uncertainty, and discomfort is where true resilience lies. Hiding your vulnerability because you're afraid of being seen as weak is like locking away your superpower because you're afraid of its potential.

### REFRAMING YOUR "WEAK" TRAITS

Let's break down some common traits that are often labeled as weaknesses and reframe them as the superpowers they really are:

1. **Sensitivity**
   Society says: You're too emotional, too fragile.
   Reality: Sensitivity is your superpower. It allows you to feel deeply, connect with others on a profound level, and tap into empathy and understanding. Sensitive people have the ability to perceive emotions and

energy that others miss. That's not weakness—it's insight.

**Superpower**: Emotional intelligence and empathy.

2. **Introversion**

   Society says: You're too quiet, too reserved, not social enough.

   Reality: Introversion gives you the ability to listen, reflect, and think deeply. You don't need to be the loudest person in the room to make an impact. In fact, **your strength lies in your quiet confidence** and ability to focus deeply on what matters to you.

   **Superpower**: Thoughtfulness, creativity, and the ability to connect deeply.

3. **Anxiety**

   Society says: You're too nervous, too cautious, too fearful.

   Reality: Anxiety, while difficult to deal with, makes you hyper-aware of potential risks and prepared for challenges. It gives you the ability to plan ahead and see potential outcomes that others might overlook. **Anxiety can make you an incredible problem-solver**.

   **Superpower**: Hyper-awareness, preparedness, and the ability to think ahead.

4. **Perfectionism**

   Society says: You're too rigid, too hard on yourself.

   Reality: While perfectionism can sometimes hold you back, it's also a reflection of your high standards and desire to do things well. When channeled in a healthy way, **your attention to detail and commitment to excellence can drive you to achieve amazing things**.

**Superpower**: Dedication, persistence, and a high standard of excellence.
5. **Empathy**
Society says: You care too much, you're too soft.
Reality: **Empathy is a superpower in a world that desperately needs more compassion**. The ability to put yourself in someone else's shoes, to feel what they're feeling, and to respond with kindness is an extraordinary strength. It allows you to build deeper connections and create positive change.
**Superpower**: Connection, compassion, and emotional intelligence.

## HOW TO TURN YOUR "WEAKNESS" INTO YOUR SUPERPOWER

Ready to start embracing your vulnerabilities as superpowers? Here's how to flip the script on perceived weakness and turn it into your greatest strength:

1. **Own Your Story**
The first step to turning your "weakness" into a superpower is to **own it**. Stop apologizing for who you are. Your sensitivity, your anxiety, your introversion—they're not things you need to hide or fix. They're part of your unique makeup, and they're what give you an edge. Own your story, flaws and all, and stop trying to fit into a version of strength that doesn't suit you.
2. **Reframe Your Narrative**
Start questioning the story you've been telling yourself about your so-called weaknesses. Are you really "too sensitive," or are you incredibly emotionally at-

tuned? Are you "too introverted," or are you deeply thoughtful? **Challenge the narrative that says these traits make you less-than**. Instead, look for the ways they've served you and how they can be your secret weapon.

3. **Embrace Vulnerability as Strength**
Vulnerability is not weakness—it's the birthplace of creativity, connection, and growth. **Stop hiding the parts of yourself that feel vulnerable** and start seeing them as sources of power. When you allow yourself to be vulnerable, you're giving others permission to do the same, and that's how real connections are built.

4. **Use Your "Weakness" to Your Advantage**
Once you've reframed your perceived weakness as a superpower, start looking for ways to use it to your advantage. For example, if you're introverted, leverage your ability to listen and think deeply in situations that require careful analysis. If you're highly sensitive, use your emotional intelligence to navigate complex relationships or difficult conversations. **Your "weakness" is an asset—learn how to use it.**

5. **Surround Yourself with People Who See Your Strength**
Not everyone will understand or appreciate your strengths, and that's okay. But it's important to surround yourself with people who value the traits that make you unique. Find friends, mentors, or colleagues who recognize your sensitivity as emotional intelligence, your introversion as deep thoughtfulness, or your empathy as powerful connection. **The**

**right people will see your superpower for what it is.**

### YOUR HOMEWORK: THE "WEAKNESS FLIP" EXERCISE

This week, I want you to try the **"Weakness Flip" Exercise**. Take one trait that you've always considered a weakness—whether it's your anxiety, sensitivity, perfectionism, or anything else—and **flip the narrative**. Write down all the ways this trait has actually served you. How has it helped you navigate challenges, connect with others, or succeed in certain areas?

Then, write down how you can start using this trait as a strength moving forward. **The goal is to reframe your "weakness" as a superpower**—and start seeing yourself as the badass you truly are.

### FINAL THOUGHT

Your vulnerabilities aren't weaknesses—they're **superpowers in disguise**. The traits you've been taught to suppress or apologize for are actually the things that make you powerful, unique, and capable of extraordinary things. **Strength doesn't come from pretending to be invincible—it comes from owning who you are, flaws and all**. So, stop hiding your so-called weaknesses and start embracing them as the superpowers they've always been. Because trust me, **you're stronger than you think**.

# 26

# THE NEED TO BE LIKED

Let's cut to the chase: **not everyone is going to like you**. And guess what? **That's a good thing**. For too long, you've probably twisted yourself into knots, tiptoeing around other people's opinions, trying to be likable, agreeable, and "perfect" in their eyes. But here's the hard truth: no matter what you do, some people just won't vibe with you—and that's okay. The problem isn't that people don't like you; it's that you're bending over backward trying to get them to.

**The need to be liked** is a deep-rooted human instinct, but when it becomes the driving force behind your decisions, it f#cks with your authenticity. You start living for other people's approval, slowly losing sight of your own needs, values, and personality. In this chapter, we're diving into why you're so obsessed with being liked, how that obsession is screwing up your happiness, and—most importantly—how to start living your best f#cking self without needing everyone to love you.

## WHY WE CRAVE APPROVAL

So, why are we so desperate for approval in the first place? It's because **being liked feels safe**. Back in the caveman days, being part of a group meant survival. Rejection wasn't just uncomfortable—it was a death sentence. Fast forward to the present, and while getting uninvited to a party won't leave you stranded in the wilderness, your brain still sees rejection as a threat. You've been wired to seek approval and validation from others because it feels like security. But here's the truth: **chasing approval isn't about safety anymore—it's about insecurity**.

Here's why you crave being liked:

1. **You Tie Your Self-Worth to Others' Opinions**
   You've convinced yourself that if people don't like you, there's something wrong with you. You've tied your self-worth to how many people approve of you, instead of building it from the inside. So, you keep jumping through hoops, thinking, *If more people like me, I'll feel good about myself.* But spoiler: **that's not how self-worth works**.
2. **You Fear Rejection**
   Rejection hurts, there's no denying it. But when you live your life avoiding rejection at all costs, you end up tiptoeing around everyone else's expectations. You become a watered-down version of yourself, so you never rock the boat or give anyone a reason to reject you. But here's the truth: **rejection isn't a death sentence—it's redirection**. It's life's way of point-

ing you toward people and situations that are actually right for you.
3. **You Want to Fit In**
Being liked feels like belonging. And who doesn't want to feel like they're part of the group? But there's a difference between authentic belonging—where you're accepted for who you are—and the fake kind of belonging that comes from trying to be what others want you to be. **Real belonging requires showing up as yourself, not as a people-pleasing version of yourself.**
4. **You've Been Conditioned to Seek Approval**
From a young age, you've been taught to follow the rules, be nice, and seek validation from authority figures, friends, family, and society at large. It's become second nature to base your actions on how much approval you'll get. But living for approval means giving up control of your own life—you're handing over the keys to your happiness to everyone else.

**THE PRICE OF BEING A PEOPLE-PLEASER**

Bending over backward for approval isn't just exhausting—it's soul-crushing. When you live your life trying to make everyone like you, **you slowly lose yourself in the process**. You start saying yes when you mean no, holding back your opinions, and reshaping your personality to fit the expectations of others. But here's what it's really costing you:

1. **You Lose Your Authenticity**
The more you try to be what others want, the more disconnected you become from who you really are.

You start hiding parts of yourself that you think won't be accepted, and eventually, you forget what it's like to show up fully and unapologetically. **Living for approval means sacrificing your authenticity—and that's a high price to pay.**

2. **You Attract the Wrong People**

When you're constantly trying to be liked, you attract people who like the version of you that's performing for approval—not the real you. This leads to shallow, unfulfilling relationships because you're too busy pleasing others to be yourself. And worse, **you miss out on the deep connections that come from being authentically you**.

3. **You Burn Yourself Out**

People-pleasing is a full-time job. You're always on high alert, scanning for cues about what people want, adjusting your behavior to meet their expectations, and feeling guilty when you don't. This sh#t is draining. **Burnout** is inevitable when you're living for other people instead of yourself.

4. **You Start Resenting the World**

When you spend your life trying to make everyone happy, you start building resentment—toward others for taking advantage of you and toward yourself for not standing up for your own needs. But the truth is, **people aren't the problem—your need for approval is**. The more you say yes when you really mean no, the more resentment builds up, until one day you explode (or implode).

## WHY NOT EVERYONE WILL LIKE YOU (AND WHY THAT'S A GOOD THING)

Here's the cold, hard truth: **not everyone is going to like you—and that's exactly how it should be**. You're not here to be universally liked, admired, or approved of. You're here to live your life on your own terms, and that means not everyone is going to be on board. And guess what? **That's a good thing**.

Here's why:

1. **Rejection Filters Out the Wrong People**
   When someone doesn't like you, they're doing you a favor. **Rejection is a filter**. It keeps the wrong people out of your life and makes space for the right people—the ones who appreciate you for who you really are. When you stop trying to please everyone, you attract the people who are genuinely aligned with you.
2. **You Can't Please Everyone**
   No matter how hard you try, you will never be able to please everyone. People have different tastes, opinions, and expectations. One person might love your boldness while another finds it off-putting. One person might admire your honesty while another sees it as too blunt. **Living for approval is a never-ending, losing battle**, because what pleases one person might piss off another.
3. **Your Self-Worth Comes from You, Not Them**
   The key to living your best f#cking self is realizing that **your self-worth comes from within**—not from how many people approve of you. When you

base your self-worth on others' opinions, you're giving them power over your happiness. Take that power back by deciding that you're worthy, no matter what anyone else thinks.

4. **Authenticity Attracts the Right Kind of Love and Respect**
People who like you for who you really are will respect you more when you stop trying to be something you're not. **Authenticity breeds respect**. When you show up as your full, imperfect self, you give others permission to do the same. And that's where real connection, love, and belonging happen.

### HOW TO STOP BENDING OVER BACKWARDS FOR APPROVAL

Ready to break free from the need to be liked and start living unapologetically? Here's how to stop chasing approval and start living for yourself:

1. **Know Your Values**
When you're clear about your values, it becomes easier to say no to the things (and people) that don't align with them. **Know what matters to you**, what you stand for, and what kind of life you want to live. When you live according to your values, you stop caring so much about what others think because you know you're living in integrity with yourself.

2. **Practice Saying No**
If you've been a chronic people-pleaser, saying no will feel uncomfortable at first—but it's necessary. Start small. **Say no to something that doesn't serve you**, whether it's a social obligation you don't want to

attend or a favor you don't have time for. Every time you say no, you're reinforcing the belief that your needs and boundaries matter.

3. **Get Comfortable with Rejection**
Rejection isn't the end of the world. In fact, it's a natural part of life. The more you get comfortable with being rejected, the less it will sting. Remember: **rejection doesn't define your worth**—it just means you weren't the right fit for that person or situation.

4. **Stop Apologizing for Being Yourself**
If you've been apologizing for who you are, it's time to stop. **Own your quirks, your imperfections, and your opinions**. You don't need to water yourself down to fit into someone else's expectations. When you stop apologizing for being yourself, you start living fully and authentically.

5. **Surround Yourself with the Right People**
The right people will love and respect you for who you are—not who you pretend to be. **Find people who appreciate your authenticity**, and let go of the ones who only like the version of you that's performing for approval. Life's too short to waste on shallow relationships.

**YOUR HOMEWORK: THE "F#CK BEING LIKED" CHALLENGE**

This week, I want you to take on the **"F#ck Being Liked" Challenge**. Pick one area of your life where you've been bending over backward for approval—whether it's at work, in a friendship, or even on social media. For one week, **stop trying to please others in that area**. Instead, focus on showing up as your true, authentic self, without worrying about how it will be received.

At the end of the week, reflect: Did the world end because you stopped caring about being liked? Did you feel more empowered, more yourself? The goal is to practice letting go of the need for approval and start living in alignment with who you really are.

**FINAL THOUGHT**

The need to be liked is a trap that keeps you from living authentically. **Not everyone will like you—and that's f#cking fantastic**. Stop bending over backward for approval, and start living your life for yourself. When you let go of the need to be liked, you make space for real connection, real belonging, and real happiness. And guess what? **The people who matter will love you even more for it**. So, go ahead—stop trying to be everyone's favorite and start being your own damn favorite.

# 27

# LACK OF MOTIVATION

We've all been there—the dreaded **rut**. That soul-sucking, energy-draining space where you feel stuck, uninspired, and completely unmotivated. Every day feels like an uphill battle, and even the simplest tasks seem impossible. You know you should be doing *something*—getting off the couch, making moves, chasing goals—but instead, you're binge-watching another episode, scrolling through social media, or procrastinating the hell out of everything. **Welcome to the sh#tty rut.**

But here's the good news: **being stuck doesn't mean you're f#cked**. You can find your drive again, even when it feels like life has turned into quicksand and you're sinking fast. This chapter is all about understanding why motivation disappears, how to reignite your fire, and how to dig yourself out of that rut—without waiting for some magical burst of energy to come out of nowhere. Spoiler alert: motivation doesn't just show up—you have to go after it.

## WHY YOU'VE LOST MOTIVATION

Before we dive into how to get your drive back, let's talk about why the hell it disappeared in the first place. **Lack of motivation** isn't laziness. It's a signal from your brain and body that something is off—whether it's burnout, lack of direction, or fear of failure. If you've lost your motivation, there's usually a reason behind it. Here's why it might have gone missing:

1. **You're Burnt Out**
   Burnout is a motivation killer. If you've been pushing yourself too hard for too long—whether it's at work, in your personal life, or even emotionally—you're going to hit a wall. **Burnout happens when you've drained yourself dry** and your body and mind hit the brakes. When you're running on empty, even the things you love feel like a chore.
2. **You're Not Excited About Your Goals**
   Let's be real: **if your goals don't excite you, they won't motivate you**. If you're chasing goals that don't align with your passions or that feel forced, it's no wonder you're not motivated to get sh#t done. When you're not emotionally connected to what you're working toward, your brain checks out, and your drive disappears.
3. **You're Afraid of Failing**
   Fear of failure can paralyze you. Sometimes it's easier to stay stuck than to risk trying and failing. **Perfectionism** and the fear of not being "good enough" often keep you in the rut. You don't want to take action because deep down, you're afraid it won't be perfect—or worse, that you'll fail altogether.

4. **You've Lost Your Purpose**
   If you're feeling stuck, it's likely because you've lost sight of your "why." When you're disconnected from your purpose—whether it's in your career, your personal life, or even just your day-to-day routines—you lose motivation. **Purpose is what gives meaning to your actions**, and without it, everything feels pointless.
5. **You're Overwhelmed**
   Sometimes the rut comes from feeling overwhelmed. You have so many things to do, so many decisions to make, that you're paralyzed by the sheer amount of sh#t on your plate. **When everything feels like too much**, motivation flies out the window, and procrastination takes its place.

**WHY WAITING FOR MOTIVATION IS A TRAP**

Here's the thing about motivation: **it doesn't just magically show up**. If you're sitting around waiting for the perfect moment when you "feel motivated," you'll be waiting forever. Motivation isn't some elusive energy that randomly appears—it's something you create through action. The more you wait for motivation to kick in, the more stuck you'll stay.

The trick is to **stop relying on motivation and start building momentum**. Taking action—even small, messy steps—creates movement. And once you're moving, motivation starts to follow. It's like lighting a fire: the flame doesn't just appear out of nowhere—you have to strike the match first.

## HOW TO DIG YOURSELF OUT OF THE RUT AND FIND YOUR DRIVE

So, how do you dig yourself out of that quicksand-like rut and find your motivation again? Here's how to tap into your drive, even when you feel like doing absolutely nothing:

1. **Start Small—Really Small**
When you're stuck, the idea of tackling big tasks feels impossible. So, **start small—really f#cking small**. Break down whatever you're avoiding into tiny, bite-sized actions. Maybe it's just writing one sentence, making one phone call, or organizing one corner of your room. Starting small creates momentum, and once you're moving, the next step becomes easier.
2. **Revisit Your "Why"**
If you've lost motivation, chances are you've lost sight of your purpose. Take a moment to reconnect with your "why." Why did you set this goal in the first place? Why does it matter? **Reignite your passion by reminding yourself of the bigger picture**. When you're connected to a purpose that lights you up, motivation starts to follow.
3. **Change Your Environment**
Sometimes the physical space you're in can contribute to your rut. If you've been slumped in the same spot for hours (or days), **shake things up**. Change your environment—whether it's going for a walk, working in a new space, or decluttering your surroundings. A shift in your physical space can spark new energy and ideas.

4. **Stop Overthinking and Just Do the Thing**
   One of the biggest motivation killers is **overthinking**. You spend so much time analyzing, worrying, and planning that you end up doing nothing. Stop overthinking and just f#cking do the thing. Even if you don't feel ready, take action anyway. You'll be surprised at how much momentum builds once you get out of your head and into action.
5. **Create a Routine (Even When You Don't Feel Like It)**
   **Routine beats motivation every time.** If you wait to "feel" motivated, you'll always have an excuse to procrastinate. But when you build a routine, you train yourself to take action whether you feel motivated or not. Create a daily routine that includes time for your goals, and stick to it. The more consistent you are, the less you'll need to rely on motivation.
6. **Set Micro-Goals and Celebrate the Wins**
   When you're in a rut, big goals feel overwhelming. Instead, set **micro-goals**—small, manageable targets you can hit in a day or even an hour. Each time you hit one, **celebrate the win**, no matter how small it seems. Celebrating progress, no matter how minor, boosts your confidence and keeps your motivation alive.
7. **Get Comfortable with Discomfort**
   Sometimes, lack of motivation is a result of avoiding discomfort. You don't want to face the hard, boring, or uncomfortable tasks, so you procrastinate instead. **Learn to embrace discomfort**. Accept that not every step will be fun or easy, but pushing through those uncomfortable moments is where growth—and motivation—happens.

### WHY YOU NEED TO DITCH PERFECTIONISM

Perfectionism is one of the biggest enemies of motivation. When you're stuck in a rut, you're often afraid to take action because you're scared it won't be perfect. But here's the thing: **perfection is a myth**. It's an excuse that keeps you from moving forward. Stop worrying about getting it "just right" and focus on getting it done. **Progress beats perfection every time**.

The more you embrace imperfection, the easier it becomes to take action. When you let go of the need to be perfect, you give yourself permission to try, fail, and keep going. And that's when motivation starts to flow.

### HOW TO KEEP THE FIRE GOING ONCE YOU'VE FOUND IT

Once you've dug yourself out of the rut and reignited your drive, the key is to keep the fire going. Here's how to maintain your momentum:

1.  **Stay Consistent**
    Consistency is what keeps motivation alive. Whether it's daily habits, regular check-ins with your goals, or setting aside time each week to work on what matters, **consistency builds momentum**. It's not about giant leaps—it's about showing up, day after day, even when you don't feel like it.
2.  **Keep Your Goals Visible**
    Don't let your goals fade into the background. Keep them front and center—write them down, create a vision board, or set daily reminders. **When your goals**

**are visible**, they stay top of mind, and it's easier to stay motivated to take action toward them.
3. **Surround Yourself with Inspiration**
   Whether it's listening to podcasts, reading books, or following people who inspire you, **surround yourself with things that keep your fire lit**. Inspiration fuels motivation, so find what speaks to you and keep it in your life.
4. **Reward Yourself Along the Way**
   Celebrate every milestone, no matter how small. **Rewards and positive reinforcement** are essential for staying motivated. Whether it's treating yourself to something special or just taking a moment to acknowledge your progress, celebrating your wins helps keep you moving forward.

**YOUR HOMEWORK: THE "JUST ONE THING" CHALLENGE**

This week, I want you to try the **"Just One Thing" Challenge**. Pick one task—just one—that you've been putting off because you're stuck in a rut. Break it down into the smallest possible step, and commit to doing **just one thing** to move it forward. Maybe it's writing one paragraph, making one phone call, or spending five minutes on a project. The goal is to get the ball rolling—because once you take that first step, motivation will follow.

At the end of the week, reflect on how it felt to take action, even when you didn't feel motivated. Did it create momentum? Did it help you get unstuck? The key is to remember that **action creates motivation—not the other way around**.

**FINAL THOUGHT**

Being stuck in a rut sucks, but it doesn't mean you're doomed to stay there forever. **Motivation isn't something you wait for—it's something you create**. By taking small steps, reconnecting with your purpose, and pushing through discomfort, you can dig yourself out of that sh#tty rut and find your drive again. Life won't always feel like fireworks and adrenaline, but when you learn to build your own momentum, you'll find that your motivation is never too far away. So stop waiting, start moving, and remember: **even the smallest step forward is still progress**.

# 28

# FEAR OF BEING YOURSELF

For most of your life, you've been wearing a mask. No, not the Halloween kind—the kind you put on every day to hide the parts of yourself you're scared for the world to see. **The fear of being yourself** is real. We all learn, at some point, that certain aspects of who we are might not be accepted by everyone. So, we shrink. We censor ourselves. We wear masks that fit into other people's expectations—hiding the messier, louder, weirder, or more vulnerable parts of ourselves. But here's the truth: **wearing that mask is exhausting**. It drains the life out of you because deep down, you know you're betraying yourself to fit in.

It's time to stop hiding. **It's time to unmask the real you**—yes, even the messy, imperfect parts you've been scared to show. This chapter is about embracing your authentic self and stepping into the world with a loud, unapologetic, "Here the f#ck I am." No more diluting yourself for other people's comfort. No more pretending to be something you're not. **Being yourself is the most pow-**

**erful thing you can do**, and it's time to stop being afraid of it.

### WHY YOU'RE SCARED TO BE YOURSELF

So, why does being your authentic self feel so terrifying? It's because **vulnerability** is scary as hell. Showing the world who you really are means exposing your flaws, insecurities, and imperfections—and there's no guarantee that people will accept you. But the real fear comes from the belief that if people don't like the real you, *then who the f#ck are you, really?*

Here's why you're afraid to let your true self out:

1.  **Fear of Rejection**
    You're terrified that if you show up as your real, unfiltered self, people will reject you. You think if they see the "real you," they won't love you, respect you, or want to be around you. The fear of rejection makes you hold back and show only the parts of yourself you think people will like. But the truth is, **being accepted for who you're pretending to be is worse than being rejected for who you really are**.
2.  **You've Been Conditioned to Fit In**
    From a young age, we're taught to conform. Fit in, follow the rules, don't rock the boat. You learn to adjust your personality, tone yourself down, and blend in to avoid standing out too much. But **fitting in doesn't equal belonging**. You can only find true belonging when you're unapologetically yourself—and that

means unlearning the need to fit into other people's expectations.

3. **Perfectionism Kicks In**
You've convinced yourself that unless you show up as the "perfect" version of yourself, you're not good enough. You're afraid of revealing your flaws, weaknesses, and struggles because perfectionism tells you those parts make you less lovable or worthy. But here's the thing: **perfection is boring as f#ck**. Your imperfections are what make you relatable, human, and, ultimately, lovable.

4. **You Don't Want to Rock the Boat**
Being yourself often means going against the grain. It means showing up with your opinions, quirks, and beliefs—even when they're not popular. And that's scary. **The fear of conflict or disapproval** keeps you playing it safe, but playing it safe is just another way of staying stuck. If you never show up as yourself, you'll never know who's truly down for you.

### THE COST OF HIDING WHO YOU ARE

The mask you've been wearing? **It's costing you big time.** When you hide parts of yourself, you're not just protecting yourself from rejection—you're also cutting yourself off from real connection, fulfillment, and self-love. Pretending to be someone you're not doesn't just drain you—it slowly eats away at your soul.

Here's what you're sacrificing by hiding who you are:

1. **You're Losing Your Authenticity**
Every time you suppress parts of yourself to fit in

or please others, you chip away at your authenticity. Over time, you lose touch with who you really are because you've been so busy performing for everyone else. **Being authentic isn't just about being "real"—it's about reclaiming your true self.**

2. **You're Settling for Shallow Relationships**

    If you're not showing up as yourself, you're attracting people who like the version of you that's performing—not the real you. This leads to shallow, unfulfilling relationships because deep down, you know you're not being seen or loved for who you really are. **Real connection happens when you're vulnerable enough to let people see the messy, imperfect parts of you.**

3. **You're Holding Yourself Back**

    Hiding your true self limits your potential. You're playing small to fit into other people's boxes, and that means you're not showing up fully in your work, relationships, or personal growth. **The world doesn't need a watered-down version of you**—it needs the real you, in all your raw, unfiltered glory.

4. **You're Blocking Your Happiness**

    True happiness comes from living authentically. When you're constantly censoring yourself, you're cutting off your joy, creativity, and freedom. **Living a life based on what others think is a sure way to end up unfulfilled and frustrated**. Happiness comes from embracing who you are—not hiding it.

**WHY BEING YOURSELF IS YOUR SUPERPOWER**

Here's the thing: **being yourself is your f#cking superpower**. The parts of you that you've been hiding—the quirks, the flaws, the weirdness—are exactly what make you unique and powerful. **There's only one you on this planet**, and that's your biggest asset. When you embrace your true self, you step into your power in a way that no one else can.

Here's why being yourself is the ultimate flex:

1. **You Attract the Right People**
   When you show up as your true self, you naturally attract people who resonate with the real you. **The right people will love you for exactly who you are**, and the wrong people will fall away. By being yourself, you're creating space for deeper, more meaningful relationships—ones that are built on authenticity, not performance.
2. **You Live Without Regret**
   Imagine looking back on your life and realizing you never showed up as your true self. That's a regret no one wants. **When you're authentic, you live without the weight of "what ifs" or missed opportunities**. You live fully, unapologetically, and on your own terms.
3. **You Free Yourself from Approval-Seeking**
   When you embrace who you are, you stop needing validation from others. You stop giving a f#ck about whether people approve of you because you've already given yourself permission to be enough. **Self-acceptance is the antidote to approval-seeking**, and it sets you free from the constant need to please.
4. **You Step Into Your Power**
   There's a special kind of power that comes from being

fully yourself. **When you stop hiding and start owning who you are**, you become unstoppable. You stop doubting yourself, second-guessing your worth, or playing small. You step into your purpose and power in a way that no one else can—because there's no competition for being the real you.

**HOW TO UNMASK THE REAL YOU AND STOP HIDING**

Ready to peel off the mask and step into your authentic self? Here's how to stop hiding and start showing up as the real you:

1. **Get to Know Yourself Again**
   If you've been wearing a mask for so long, you might have lost touch with who you really are. **Take time to reconnect with yourself**. What do you love? What makes you weird, quirky, or unique? What are your values, passions, and non-negotiables? The more you get to know yourself, the easier it becomes to show up as your true self.
2. **Practice Radical Self-Acceptance**
   The key to being yourself is accepting yourself first. **Radical self-acceptance** means embracing all of who you are—the flaws, the strengths, the insecurities, and the greatness. Stop trying to "fix" yourself and start seeing your imperfections as part of your unique makeup.
3. **Start Small but Honest**
   You don't have to unmask everything overnight. **Start small** by being honest in situations where you'd normally hide or hold back. Speak your mind, show your quirks, or share something vulnerable with

someone you trust. The more you practice being real, the easier it becomes to drop the mask entirely.
4. **Stop Giving a F#ck About What Others Think**
Not everyone is going to like the real you—and that's okay. **The more you stop giving a f#ck about other people's opinions**, the freer you'll feel to be yourself. Your job isn't to please everyone; it's to live authentically. People's opinions aren't your business, and they don't define your worth.
5. **Find Your Tribe**
Surround yourself with people who encourage you to be your true self—people who love and accept you for who you are, not who you pretend to be. **Your tribe will celebrate your authenticity, not judge it.** When you're surrounded by the right people, it becomes easier to drop the mask and show up fully.

**YOUR HOMEWORK: THE "UNMASKING" EXERCISE**

This week, I want you to try the **Unmasking Exercise**. Pick one area of your life where you've been hiding—whether it's at work, in your relationships, or even in your creative pursuits. **Take one bold step toward being your true self** in that area. Maybe it's speaking your mind in a meeting, sharing a piece of your writing, or showing your quirky side to friends. Whatever it is, make it a conscious choice to unmask the real you.

At the end of the week, reflect on how it felt to show up authentically. Was it terrifying? Liberating? Did it bring you closer to people or help you feel more aligned with yourself? The goal is to practice showing up as the real you—little by little—until it becomes second nature.

**FINAL THOUGHT**

The fear of being yourself is rooted in the belief that you're not enough as you are—but that's a f#cking lie. **You are more than enough**, and the world needs the real, unapologetic you to show up. It's time to unmask the parts of yourself you've been hiding, step into your authenticity, and tell the world, **"Here the f#ck I am."** Because the truth is, there's no one else who can be you—and that's your greatest superpower.

# 29

# SAYING F#CK IT

There's a kind of magic that happens when you finally decide to stop giving a f#ck. Suddenly, all the things that used to stress you out, hold you back, or make you doubt yourself don't seem so important anymore. **Saying "f#ck it" is the ultimate power move**, and it's the key to unlocking a life where you're free from other people's opinions, unnecessary stress, and endless self-doubt. **When you give fewer f#cks, you gain more freedom.** It's that simple.

The problem is, we live in a world that teaches us to care about *everything*—what people think of us, how we measure up to others, what society expects, whether we're successful enough, attractive enough, likable enough. **We're drowning in f#cks**, and it's exhausting. But here's the secret: **you don't have to care about everything.** In fact, the less you care about the stuff that doesn't matter, the more energy you'll have for the stuff that actually does.

This chapter is about learning the fine art of giving fewer f#cks. It's about cutting through the noise, identifying what's really worth your time and energy, and letting go of the rest. Because once you start saying "f#ck it," you take back control of your life—and trust me, that's the ultimate power move.

**WHY YOU'RE GIVING TOO MANY F#CKS**

So, why are you giving so many f#cks in the first place? **You've been conditioned to care about way too much.** From a young age, we're taught that other people's opinions matter—a lot. Whether it's making sure you're "likable" at school, meeting your parents' expectations, or trying to keep up with society's impossible standards, the message is clear: care, care, care.

But here's the problem: **the more you care about everything, the less you actually enjoy your life.** You end up stressed, overwhelmed, and constantly trying to meet someone else's standards. **Not everything deserves your time, energy, or attention**, and caring about the wrong things leaves you drained, frustrated, and burned out.

Here's why you're giving too many f#cks:

1. **You're a People-Pleaser**
   You've been taught that other people's approval matters more than your own happiness. So, you spend your life trying to please everyone else, giving a f#ck about every opinion, request, and expectation thrown your way. But guess what? **People-pleasing is a one-way ticket to misery.** You'll never make everyone happy, and trying to will only leave you exhausted.

2. **You're Afraid of Judgment**
   The fear of being judged keeps you stuck in a cycle of caring way too much about what others think. You worry that if you don't care enough, people will think you're selfish, lazy, or not good enough. But here's the truth: **people are going to judge you no matter what**—so you might as well do what makes you happy.
3. **You're Chasing Perfection**
   Perfectionism is a trap that convinces you to care about every little detail, every outcome, and every possible mistake. But here's the thing: **perfection is an illusion.** The more you chase it, the more you care about things that don't actually matter, like whether your life looks picture-perfect to the outside world. Spoiler: it doesn't need to.
4. **You're Living by Other People's Rules**
   Society has a lot of unspoken rules about what you *should* care about: success, appearances, status, fitting in. But living by someone else's rules means you're constantly giving f#cks about things that don't align with your values. **It's time to make your own rules.**

**THE FREEDOM OF GIVING FEWER F#CKS**

When you stop giving so many f#cks, something incredible happens: **you get your life back**. Suddenly, all the things that used to keep you up at night—the opinions of others, the fear of failure, the pressure to be perfect—lose their grip on you. You realize that most of the sh#t you've been stressing over doesn't actually matter.

**And the stuff that does? You have more energy to focus on it**.

Here's what happens when you give fewer f#cks:

1. **You Stop Wasting Energy**
   Giving a f#ck about everything is draining. **You only have so much energy**, and when you waste it on things that don't matter—like worrying about what people think or trying to meet ridiculous standards—you have nothing left for what actually matters. When you stop caring about the wrong things, you free up energy to focus on the stuff that lights you up.
2. **You Start Living Authentically**
   The less you care about what others think, the more freedom you have to live your life on your own terms. **Authenticity happens when you stop giving a f#ck about other people's expectations** and start caring about what feels right for you. You stop pretending to be someone you're not and start embracing who you really are.
3. **You Reduce Stress and Anxiety**
   A lot of your stress and anxiety comes from caring about things that aren't worth it—like what people will think, whether you're doing everything "right," or if you're measuring up. But when you start saying "f#ck it," you let go of that stress. **You realize that most of the pressure you feel is self-imposed**, and you don't have to carry it.
4. **You Focus on What Really Matters**
   Giving fewer f#cks isn't about not caring about *anything*—it's about caring deeply about the right things.

When you stop wasting energy on sh#t that doesn't matter, you have more space to focus on what actually matters to you, whether that's your relationships, your passions, your health, or your happiness.

**THE ART OF SAYING F#CK IT: HOW TO MASTER IT**

Ready to master the art of giving fewer f#cks? Here's how to start saying "f#ck it" to the things that don't matter and reclaim your energy, time, and peace of mind:

1.  **Identify Your F#cks**
    The first step is getting clear on what you've been giving too many f#cks about. **Make a list of all the things you're currently stressing over**, from people's opinions to your to-do list to societal expectations. Then, ask yourself: *Does this really matter? Is this worth my energy?* If the answer is no, it's time to let it go.
2.  **Set Your F#ck Priorities**
    Once you've identified what doesn't matter, get clear on what *does*. **What's truly important to you?** What are your core values? What are the things you actually want to give a f#ck about? Focus your energy on those things and let the rest fall away. The key is to care deeply about the things that light you up—and stop wasting f#cks on everything else.
3.  **Practice Saying No**
    Learning to say "no" is one of the most powerful ways to give fewer f#cks. **You don't have to say yes to everything or everyone**. When something doesn't align with your priorities, give yourself permission to

say no without guilt. Saying no isn't selfish—it's an act of self-respect.

4. **Stop Seeking Validation**

One of the biggest reasons you give too many f#cks is because you're seeking validation from others. **But here's the truth: no one's approval matters more than your own**. The more you stop seeking validation, the freer you'll feel. Validate yourself, trust your instincts, and let go of the need for outside approval.

5. **Let Go of Perfectionism**

Perfectionism is the enemy of saying "f#ck it." **The more you chase perfection, the more f#cks you give about things that don't matter**—like how others perceive you or whether you're doing things "right." Let go of the need to be perfect and embrace the beauty of imperfection. Progress is more important than perfection, and when you stop giving a f#ck about getting everything "just right," you free yourself to actually get sh#t done.

6. **Embrace Discomfort**

Saying "f#ck it" means getting comfortable with discomfort. You're going to face moments where people don't like your decisions, where you feel uncertain, or where you worry about judgment. But here's the thing: **discomfort is temporary—freedom is forever**. The more you embrace the discomfort of not giving a f#ck, the easier it gets.

**YOUR HOMEWORK: THE "F#CK IT LIST" CHALLENGE**

This week, I want you to create your own **"F#ck It List."** Sit down and write out all the things you've been giving too many f#cks about lately—whether it's people's opinions, unnecessary obligations, or unrealistic expectations. **Then, cross out the ones that aren't worth your time or energy anymore.** Once you've crossed them off, practice letting go of those things in real life.

At the end of the week, reflect on how it felt to give fewer f#cks. Did you feel lighter? Less stressed? More in control of your own life? The goal is to start cutting out the noise and focusing on what really matters to you—because that's where your power lies.

**FINAL THOUGHT**

Saying "f#ck it" is the ultimate power move because it frees you from the weight of caring about sh#t that doesn't matter. **The fewer f#cks you give, the more space you create for the things that truly matter**—the things that align with your values, your joy, and your growth. So, stop wasting your energy on approval-seeking, perfectionism, and stress. **Master the art of saying "f#ck it," and you'll find the freedom you've been looking for all along.**

# THE FINAL F#CK

Well, here you are. You've journeyed through the raw, messy, hilarious, and downright uncomfortable landscape of your insecurities, fears, and self-doubt. You've looked your sh#t in the face, laughed at it, learned from it, and now you're standing on the other side. **Welcome to Fear-LESSence—the art of not giving a f#ck**. It's not just a catchy phrase or a mindset to flirt with once in a while. It's a way of life—a way of unapologetically **owning who you are**, ditching the bullsh#t that weighs you down, and living on your terms.

You've spent too long caring about all the wrong things—whether it's what people think, the fear of failure, or the crippling pressure to be perfect. **Life's too f#cking short to care so damn much.** It's time to let that sh#t go. You're not here to tiptoe around, seeking approval or trying to fit into everyone else's expectations. You're here to **live boldly, authentically, and without apology**.

### THE FEARLESSENCE MANTRA: GIVE FEWER F#CKS

Here's the bottom line: **you don't need to be liked by everyone, succeed at everything, or live a life that's perfectly polished.** You need to be true to yourself, embrace your imperfections, and stop giving a f#ck about things that don't matter. The FearLESSence mindset isn't about being reckless or not caring at all—it's about **caring selectively**. It's about giving your energy, time, and heart to the people, goals, and values that actually light you up—and letting go of the rest.

You've learned how to face your fears, silence your inner critic, and stop chasing approval. You've learned that failure isn't the end of the world, that vulnerability is strength, and that you deserve to live without the weight of guilt, shame, or judgment. **You've unmasked the real you—and damn, that version of you is unstoppable.**

### EMBRACE YOUR FEARLESSENCE

So what now? **Now, you live it.** You wake up every day and choose to embrace your FearLESSence. You stop bending over backward for approval. You stop letting fear of failure or rejection dictate your actions. You show up, flaws and all, and you say, "Here the f#ck I am." You give fewer f#cks about the things that don't matter, and you go all-in on what does.

You embrace your quirks, your weirdness, your mistakes, your brilliance. You stop apologizing for taking up space, and you start claiming your life as your own. **You realize that you're already enough, just as you are.**

### THE FREEDOM OF FEARLESSENCE

Here's the beauty of living with FearLESSence: **it's liberating as hell.** When you stop caring so much about everything that doesn't matter, you free yourself. Free to take risks, free to fail, free to laugh at your own sh#t, free to live without the crushing weight of expectations.

Life is going to throw you challenges, doubts, and curveballs. That's a guarantee. But with FearLESSence, you'll face them with humor, resilience, and a newfound strength that comes from knowing you don't have to be perfect or have it all figured out. **You just have to show up and live the f#ck out of your life.**

### THE FINAL F#CK

You've done the work, you've read the chapters, and now it's time for the final f#ck: **the f#ck you stop giving about anything that doesn't serve you.** FearLESSence is about living boldly, unapologetically, and fully in the present. It's about owning who you are without trying to change for anyone else. It's about embracing the messiness, the mistakes, and the magic of being human.

So, here's your last piece of advice: **stop giving a f#ck about what doesn't matter, and go live your damn life.** Because you, my friend, are more than enough. You always have been. Now, it's time to believe it and live it. **FearLESSence is yours to claim—so go out there and f#cking own it.**